Derbyshire's Unsung Heroes

Derbyshire's Unsung Heroes

Malcolm Cowper

First published in Great Britain in 2013 by

Bannister Publications Ltd
118 Saltergate
Chesterfield
Derbyshire S40 1NG

ISBN 978-1-909813-00-7

Malcolm Cowper asserts his moral right
to be identified as the author of this work

A catalogue record for this book is available from the British Library

Typeset in Palatino Linotype and designed by Escritor Design
Chesterfield, Derbyshire

Printed and bound in the UK by SRP Ltd, Exeter

bannister●
publications

To Duncan and Simon, my sons and my best friends.

CONTENTS

Foreword

The idea for this book came to me one day when, out of idle curiosity, I was skimming through the obituary columns of my local paper. Each had a brief biography, and my attention was drawn to sentences such as 'Served in the Royal Navy during the war' or 'Did war service in the Land Army', and it occurred to me that behind these terse statements there must be many untold stories of life during that extraordinary period between 1939 and 1945.

There have been plenty of wars since, but no generation has had to experience total war, where the life of every man, woman and child was affected. Thousands have written of their experiences during those years, but many more have not, and time is running out to capture these memories.

I wrote to several local papers asking anyone with memories of wartime life to contact me. The response was extraordinary, and over the next few weeks my phone rang frequently as more and more people said they had a story to tell. Some had served in the armed forces, some had worked in the factories, down the mines or on the land, some had been children with memories of nights spent in shelters during bombing raids.

Interviewing them was fascinating, and I came to realise what an extraordinary generation they were, and how much we owe them for their fortitude and their resilience in the face of one of the most barbaric and ruthless enemies this country has ever had to face.

I have called this book 'Derbyshire's Unsung Heroes' (even though some of the contributors live just over the border in Nottinghamshire) because in my view they were all heroes and heroines. Very few of them actually received any medals, or even any official recognition, but they all bravely and uncomplainingly, and often at great personal sacrifice, went about the task of winning the war. And when the job was done they set about building a better world for us, their children.

I dedicate this book to them, in admiration and gratitude.

Malcolm Cowper
February 2013

INTRODUCTION

Until 1914, wars were usually fought by volunteer soldiers and sailors in faraway places. While they were away, the women and children got on with their normal lives safely at home, and waited in the hope that their menfolk would come back alive and in one piece.

All that changed in the First World War, for although the land fighting took place overseas, the arrival of the bomber aircraft meant that the women and children were no longer safe. Although the number of bombs that were dropped on this country (mainly London) was minute compared with that in the next war, the terror that this new weapon brought was out of all proportion to the damage done. Furthermore, the appalling casualty rate on the Western Front meant that in 1916 conscription had to be introduced as the flow of volunteers for the army dried up, and for the first time women were required to work in the factories to replace the men that had been called up.

Although 1914-18 was described as 'the war to end wars', by the mid-1930s it was becoming obvious that there was going to be a Second World War, and reluctantly the government began to make plans for it. As soon as it did break out in 1939 conscription was introduced and children were evacuated from cities at risk of bombing to safer areas in the country. Soon women were once again being recruited into the factories and on to the farms, and men too old or too young to serve in the forces joined the Home Guard, or became Air Raid Wardens or Firewatchers. Later in the war men were conscripted into the mines to meet the insatiable demand for coal, and women as well as men were called up for service in the armed forces. Scouts and Guides went round doing useful jobs such as salvaging scrap to be recycled into war materials. Everybody was expected to 'do their bit'.

The threat of invasion was very real, and throughout the summer of 1940 the country braced itself for invasion by the mighty, all-conquering German army. However, the fierce resistance of the RAF against the vast armadas of enemy bombers over England eventually forced Hitler to postpone, and finally abandon, the invasion. With this threat removed, the population settled down to the changed circumstances that war had brought to their lives and doggedly continued to contend with rationing, shortages, blackouts, bombing raids and the absence of their loved ones serving overseas.

They turned their gardens into allotments and grew vegetables to supplement their meagre rations. As their clothes wore out they 'made do and mended' until they had enough coupons to replace them, although there was no guarantee that new clothes would be available when they did. They worked long hours in the factories and on the farms, and when they came home exhausted at the end of they day they might well have to go out all night fire-watching or on Home Guard duty. They did all this without whingeing or moaning. They just 'got on with the job'.

When victory came in 1945 they were jubilant but utterly exhausted. The rest of the decade offered little respite from the hardships of rationing, which actually became more severe than during the war. The bombs no longer dropped, the lights were back on, families long separated were reunited but life continued to be a struggle, and not only in a material sense. Marriages were put under intense strain as the men who returned in 1945 were no longer the men who had gone off in 1939. War had changed them, and they did not find it easy to settle back into civilian life. Women who had worked and enjoyed the independence of earning their own money did not willingly return to the kitchen sink. Children who had grown up in all-female households were resentful of the strange man whom they had to call 'Daddy' and who was now the head of the household. The divorce rate spiralled.

On the positive side, this generation was determined that after the titanic struggle and the enormous sacrifices they were going to create a better, fairer world. Much as they revered Winston Churchill for his inspirational leadership during the war, they knew he was not the man to build the kind of world they now wanted. Instead, they voted in Clement Atlee's Labour government, which despite the country's massive debts, set about building houses and schools, and creating a National Health Service so that everyone, regardless of social class, should have decent homes, free education and free healthcare 'from the cradle to the grave.' Eventually, as the country got back on its feet, austerity gave way to affluence and the rest of the twentieth century saw prosperity rise to unprecedented levels.

We owe so much to this remarkable generation, and now, as they approach the evening of their lives, we must never forget what they achieved. This is why it was important to me to give the remaining veterans of the war in my local area of Derbyshire the chance to tell their stories, so that we who have never lived through a war know how it completely affected their lives. This book is not an attempt to glorify war, but to try to show what it was like for ordinary people living through extraordinary times, when normal life was put on hold and they found themselves enduring what no subsequent generation in this country has had to endure.

I have divided these stories into four sections. 'The Call to Arms' is about the men and women who served in the armed forces; 'The Home Front' deals with the civilians who provided the essential backup to the fighting services; 'Wartime Childhoods' tells of the experiences of children who had to cope with all the dangers and hardships of war at a very young age; and 'National Service', which was introduced after the war, but came about as a direct result of it.

Derbyshire's Unsung Heroes

THE CALL TO ARMS

All men between the ages of 18 and 45, unless in a reserved occupation such as farming or coal mining, or unless medically unfit, were required to serve in the armed forces from being called up till the end of the war (and often beyond that). Those who did not wish to do so could register as conscientious objectors, usually on religious grounds, but were still required to do war work of some sort such as forestry or agriculture. If they refused to do this they could be sent to prison, but far fewer were imprisoned for this reason than in the First World War.

In any case, there were considerable social pressures to join up, and a young and apparently fit young man in 'civvies' could be the object of comments to the effect that he was shirking his duty, although no white feathers were handed out by young women as in the previous war. And although there was not the mad rush to volunteer as there had been in 1914, many young men decided to do so before they were called up so as to at least have some choice as to the branch of the forces they served in.

Most of the former soldiers I interviewed had been barely out of their teens when they had their first experience of the horrors of war on the beaches of Normandy as part of the D-Day landings in June 1944, and over the following months of bitter fighting had slowly but surely pushed the Germans back into their homeland. During that time they had to contend not only with the fierce resistance of the enemy but also the bitter cold of one of the worst winters of the century. After the defeat of Germany in May 1945, instead of going home many of them found themselves having to police a lawless country where gangs of recently released slave workers set about wreaking revenge on their tormentors, and it was well into 1947 before some finally came home.

The men who served at sea were mainly engaged in ensuring that Britain and its allies were kept supplied in essential food and war materials. As a defence against the predatory German submarines (U-boats), merchant ships had to travel in convoys protected by warships of the Royal Navy. Their battle was against the relentless attacks of the U-boats and enemy bombers as well as the freezing weather and the often ferocious seas of the North Atlantic and Arctic oceans. The constant fear of death by explosion or drowning must have put an enormous strain on these men.

The role of the RAF was both to defend the country against air attacks and to take the war to the enemy in the form of bombing raids. One of the men I interviewed was highly successful in shooting down German bombers at night and won the DFC no less than four times (three British, one American). The other, after an extremely brief flying career, suffered the fate of many aircrew by being shot down and spending the war incarcerated in a prison camp, where he helped in the organisation of the mass break-out that was later immortalised in the film 'The Great Escape'.

Two of the service personnel I interviewed were women. One was a driver in the Women's Auxiliary Air Force (WAAF), and witnessed a terrible crash on the airfield, the other served in the ATS (Auxiliary Territorial Service, the women's army) decoding enemy signals at Bletchley Park, headquarters of a team of brilliant scientists and mathematicians without whose work the war may never have been won.

When the war was over all these people had to pick up the pieces of their pre-war lives and, without the aid of Post Traumatic Stress Counselling, put all their experiences, however horrific, behind them and get on with the business of being civilians again.

John Bamford

Corporal in the Gordon Highlanders

When John Bamford suddenly found himself face-to-face with an armed German soldier, he did not hesitate for a second. He raised his rifle and shot him The fact that this was someone's son, father or husband did not enter his head. Yet John was no murderer. In civilian life he would have been appalled at the prospect of killing another man; but as a soldier in battle those standards of human decency had no place. A moment's hesitation and John would have been the one to fall to the ground.

Like thousands of others, John, from Worksop, had been plucked from his peacetime job as an office boy, put into uniform and trained to be a killer. Not that he had any hatred of Germans. As he put it, "Your enemy was the uniform, not the man." Ironically, however, it had not been his original intention to join the army. Having been a cadet in the Air Training Corps, where he became proficient at Morse Code, he had wanted to join the RAF as a wireless operator/air gunner. However, when he applied in June 1943, aged seventeen and a half, he was told to come back when he was nineteen. Fearing that the war would be over by then, he applied to the army and was immediately accepted.

Though he had no connection whatsoever with Scotland, John was assigned to the Gordon Highlanders and did his training with the Black Watch. His active service began in August 1944 when the Highlanders crossed the Channel to Normandy. Two months after D Day, the Allies had fought their way to Falaise, where they were held up by fierce resistance from the Germans.

It was here that John had a near-fatal encounter with the enemy. With thirty-three other members of 17 Platoon he was crossing the River Seine in a canvas boat when suddenly, half way across, they came under deadly fire. They immediately turned back, but fourteen men were killed, twelve wounded, and John was only one of seven

Close house-to-house fighting in Kleve 1945. John Bamford is front centre if this press picture

to get back unharmed. The memory that haunts him to this day is the sight of the water red with blood.

As the front line slowly advanced through Belgium and into Holland, conditions for the troops became appalling as one of the harshest winters of the century set in. In freezing conditions they had to sleep in two-man slit trenches, where they had no protection whatsoever from the cold. They tried to keep warm as best they could with greatcoats, groundsheets and blankets, and John used straw from a nearby barn to put round his feet. They dared not raise their heads above ground level for fear of being shot by snipers. They had to live on field rations, known as 'hard tack', so called because the domino-sized biscuits were so hard it was impossible to eat them without soaking them first. Tea was brewed in mess tins on portable 'Tommy Cookers'. After several days, sometimes longer, they would be relieved and return, exhausted, to the comparative comfort of a rest camp, where they could wash, shave and catch up on sleep. For John a major hardship on the front line was not being able to clean his teeth! He would rub them so vigorously with his finger that he would end up loosening them.

Die Folgen der Rheinlandoffensive, die die Alliierten mit mehr als einer Million Soldaten führten, dokumentiert dieses Foto, das Goch 1945 zeigt.

A cutting from a German publication shows Allied troops moving through Kleve, 1945

When the Germans tried to break through in the Ardennes, the Highlanders were went to provide reinforcements. As they approached, they encountered American soldiers running in the opposite direction! They carried on forwards and the Germans, overwhelmed by superior numbers, were driven back.

By February 1945 John's unit had reached the town of Kleve, in northern Germany near the Dutch border, which was almost completely destroyed by artillery and bombing. Mopping up operations were highly dangerous, as you never knew where the enemy was hiding. Evacuated buildings were full of booby traps such as pens or watches, which would explode on being picked up. The local civilians were suffering terribly. On one occasion John gave some soap to a woman who had seen none for weeks, and she could not have been more grateful if he had offered her a handful of diamonds!

It was near Kleve, at the Schloss Kalbeck, that John shot the German who suddenly appeared in front of him as he was entering the building to get a better view from upstairs. He then ran upstairs to the first floor, kicked open the door of the first room he came to, only to find five German soldiers in there. However, although they were all armed they immediately put their hands up in surrender! John shouted downstairs for his sergeant and they escorted their prisoners into captivity.

John's fighting war came to an abrupt end on the day before his nineteenth birthday. They were now in the Reichswald, a dense forest, eerily quiet. Suddenly John felt a searing pain in his right leg as it was struck by a piece of shrapnel, which severed the bone. He passed out, and was sedated by morphine for the next few days as he was taken back to 'Blighty', and when he woke up he was in Morriston Hospital, near Swansea. An operation failed to remove all the shrapnel, and some remained embedded in his leg for the rest of his life. He spent the next nine months learning to walk again, and it was several years before he lost the stiffness in his leg.

Because he had joined up comparatively late in the war, John had to wait until 1947 before he was demobilised. Until then he was stationed at the York Demobilisation Centre with the rank of corporal, in charge of issuing railway warrants to personnel going on leave. This made him very popular, especially with senior NCOs, who made sure he did not get weekend duties in return for him facilitating their travel arrangements!

When he did come home, John found it hard to adjust to civilian life. Although his period of active service was comparatively short, he had been just a teenager when he witnessed horrific scenes of slaughter, and the memories are still painful to this day. He told me that he had never talked about his wartime experiences before, and was close to tears at times. Like most men of his generation, it did not come easily to talk about his feelings. There was no post-traumatic stress counselling for them; they were expected to 'get on with it' and put it all behind them. But horrific memories can never be totally expurgated. They remain buried in the deepest recesses of the mind, ready to surface when you least expect it. Like the other ex-servicemen that I interviewed, it is only now, when many years have passed, that he was able to talk about his memories, and I felt that for him, as for others, it was a relief to do so.

Jim Liggatt

Sergeant in the Royal Marines

When Jim Liggatt told his father he was going to join the Marines, the response he got was "You'll never be good enough!" Having served in the Marines himself during the First World War, where he saw action at Gallipoli, Mr Liggatt senior knew how tough the training was. But Jim was determined to prove him wrong, and on 30 September 1942, two months before his eighteenth birthday, he also became a Marine.

Based at Chatham, Jim went through five months of the most rigorous training. At times he wondered if his father might have been right, but he stuck it out, determined to prove that he was good enough. The training included a weekly route march, which increased in length each week. The first was five miles, then ten, fifteen, twenty, and finally twenty-five. The last two were done in full kit and carrying a full complement of weapons: Bren gun and two magazines of ammunition, mortar and two bombs, and four hand grenades! "We were exhausted and bow-legged by the time we got back to Chatham," said Jim. To finish off this arduous training they had to march thirty miles a day for six days, sleeping in church or village halls en route. To Jim's surprise, their final destination was his home town of Chesterfield. To his intense frustration, however, he was not allowed to visit his family, who had no idea he was there!

Having completed his basic training, Jim was sent to Achnagarry, in Scotland, for six weeks commando training. Here he had the first of a series of accidents which resulted in his being treated for wounds before he even got to grips with the enemy. He was going down the much-feared 'death slide' but as he reached the bottom he landed heavily and broke his ankle. This put an end to his commando training, as total fitness was required for this role.

He was sent to Poole, in Dorset, and it was while he was there that

Sgt Jim Liggard, Royal Marines

he found himself unexpectedly in the presence of royalty! He and a few mates were walking into town one evening, there being no buses, when a large Daimler flying the royal pennant drew up and the chauffeur asked if they wanted a lift. The occupant of the car was none other than Queen Mary, widow of the late King George V, who like to give lifts to servicemen as her contribution to the war effort! Having been instructed to address her as 'Ma'am', they chatted with her until they reached their destination. When they got out they stood in a line and saluted her, and she gave them a regal wave as she drove off.

Further accidents, either as a result of carelessness or just plain stupidity, occurred to Jim over the next few months. Whilst they were on the rifle range another Marine, believing his gun to be empty, pulled the trigger. It was still loaded and the bullet hit the floor before part of it went into the back of Jim's leg. On another occasion a sleepy American sentry guarding a ship fired at him in the fog. Jim threw himself on the ground, and his rifle fell into the dock and had to be retrieved by a Naval diver.

In January 1944, Jim suffered yet another injury while on exercise off the South Coast on a landing craft. Live ammunition was being fired, and a shell from a nearby ship just missed him but injured both his hands. He was sent home to Chesterfield where a piece of lead was removed from his hand. Having some free time, he decided to call in at Robinsons, his former employer, where they had a servicemen's fund. He was given ten shillings, but this was not the only benefit from his visit. While he had worked there he had been attracted to a young lady called Ruth, but he had never had the courage to ask her out. She felt the same way towards him, and seeing him there that day she decided that unless she took the initiative they might never get together. So she said, "There's a very good film on at the Regal this week. Would you like to take me to see it?" Jim eagerly agreed and that was the start of a relationship that would last for sixty-six years!

Jim went into action in June 1944 supporting the D-Day landings on Gold Beach. (Each of the Normandy beaches was given a code name: Gold, Juno, Sword, Omaha and Utah). He was a crew member of an LCF, an armoured landing craft, and their job was to support the infantry by shelling enemy shore batteries from the sea. It was relentless work, and it was not until nightfall that they were able to relax and have a hot drink and some food. They had not eaten since four that morning.

After three weeks, during which Jim had fired over four thousand 40mm shells, their job was done, but before they could cross back to England they had to go ashore for a few days to strengthen a defence position so that a commando brigade could rest, rearm and get some proper food. The following morning the Germans counter-attacked but were beaten back and lost over two hundred men.

Jim then got five days leave. Back in England, he and his mates tried to board a train but it was full. Determined to get home for these precious few days, they sat themselves down on the line in front of the train and refused to move! The furious station master intervened, but when the men made it known that they were back from Normandy and had only five days leave his attitude changed completely. One carriage was vacated voluntarily so that the men could have it to themselves. Beer and sandwiches appeared and for the rest of the journey they were treated like royalty!

Jim was utterly exhausted, having had hardly any sleep for a month. However, on his way home he called in at Robinsons to see Ruth, and arranged to meet her that evening after he had had a sleep. However, he fell into such a deep sleep that nobody, not even Ruth, could wake him, and she spent her date sitting by his bedside! When he had not woken by the next morning his mother became seriously worried and insisted on calling the doctor, who assured her that he was just totally exhausted. Finally, after thirty hours asleep, he woke. Now fully recovered, he lost no time in meeting up again with Ruth. He raided his savings, bought a £10 gold ring and proposed to her. To his delight, she accepted.

However, before they could marry he had to go back to Normandy. Their job now was to protect the eastern flank of Gold Beach from attack by E Boats (fast armed patrol boats) and EMBs, motor boats with an explosive charge in the bow. These would be aimed at a ship by a man who would set the charge, rev it up to full speed, then bail out on a float and hope to be picked up out of the water.

In September 1944 Jim got leave to get married. They decided not to wait for the end of the war in case Jim did not come back. In fact, he very nearly didn't. It was often said that you never heard the shell that was going to get you, and Jim never heard the one that exploded right by him a few weeks later off the coast of Holland. The blast knocked him several feet across the deck. His face was badly injured, his nose was broken and his eardrums were pierced. He also had two pieces of shrapnel in his leg. Several of the crew were killed, and Jim was believed to be dead, but though badly injured, he was still alive.

The LCF was severely damaged, but managed to limp back over the next three days to Portsmouth. Jim was placed under medical supervision while his face recovered. When he was fit again he was promoted to corporal and sent to Wales to train in the new LCFs in preparation for service in the Far East. Although the end of the war in Europe was now only weeks away, Japan was far from finished and preparations were being made to send troops to the Far East to reinforce our forces out there. However, the dropping of the atomic bombs on Hiroshima and Nagasaki in August brought the war to a sudden and unexpected end.

However, it would be another year before Jim was able to return to civilian life, and he spent this time in the pay and records office dealing with demobilisations. Later he was promoted to sergeant and became Guard Commander in the Devon seaside town of Ilfracombe. In this role he received two commendations, one for preventing some unruly youths from entering a dance hall and causing trouble, and one for arresting a suspected rapist.

A Landing Craft Flak (LCF) pictured in 1944. The craft had a crew of about 50 Royal Marines and was typically armed with up to 12 or more light anti-aircraft guns.

Jim was finally demobilised in June 1946, and at last was able to settle down with his beloved Ruth. However, he remained as a paid reservist for the next eight years, and was actually called up during the Korean War (1950-53), but to his and Ruth's relief he was never sent there. He would have needed three months re-training, and by the time he got to Korea the war would have been nearly over. Had he gone, he would almost certainly never have come back, as the Marines sustained nearly 100% casualties there.

Asked what was his abiding memory of his war service, Jim recalled the intense fear on the eve of D-Day when the officer commanding his ship said, "By this time tomorrow you might all be dead." To a young man barely out of his teens, with his whole life in front of him and soon to be married, these were chilling words. Another of his fears was of being badly wounded and suffering intense pain. This, he thought, would be worse than dying.

At the end of the interview, Jim echoed the sentiments of the other men who had been in battle, that the terrible memories remain with you all your life. "You can never forget the war. It never goes away," he said, but added "I wouldn't have missed it for the world." This may seem strange, given the horrors he had been through, but at the same time he would have experienced the intense comradeship of men facing death and relying on each other to survive.

Jim had proved his father wrong. Not only had he been good enough to be a Marine, but he had actually done better, for he ended his four years service as a sergeant whereas his father had still held the lowest rank after the same period of time!

Neville Dean

Driver and Instructor
in the Royal Tank Regiment

Most soldiers witnessed unspeakable horrors on the battlefield. Such sights were seared into their memories, there to remain for the rest of their lives, impossible to forget no matter how hard they tried to bury them. A few, however, were witnesses to horrors even more appalling than on the battlefield, sights for which nothing in their previous experience had prepared them.

Neville Dean was a tank driver. In April 1945, advancing into Germany and with the end of the war just a month away, his unit was ordered to take flame-thrower tanks into what they believed was a prisoner-of-war camp and incinerate the huts, as there had been an outbreak of typhus. As they approached the camp they became aware of a sickening smell, unlike anything they had ever known. What they saw as they entered the camp can only be described as a vision of hell.

All around them were piles of corpses, naked and emaciated. In among them living skeletons shuffled aimlessly. This was no prisoner-of-war camp but Belsen-Bergen, one of the notorious Nazi death camps. It had been liberated a few days earlier by Canadian troops, who were trying to do what they could for the traumatised survivors. Food was what they desperately craved, but the troops had to be extremely careful only to give them small amounts, for to put too much into their shrunken stomachs would have killed them.

Thirty thousand had died of disease and starvation in the months leading up to the liberation, including Ann Frank, whose diary of her family's ordeal in hiding from the Nazis in an attic in Amsterdam would become a world best seller. Despite the best efforts of their liberators, a further ten thousand would die, their bodies too weakened to survive. At least during their last days and weeks they would have experienced the forgotten sensation of kindness and care instead of brutality and abuse.

Over the next few weeks the pictures of these places of horror would be seen around the world, but for Neville no film could adequately convey the hideousness of what he had witnessed, and it remains to this day his worst memory of the war.

Neville was born in the Derbyshire village of Kirk Ireton. He became an apprentice bricklayer after leaving school, and in July 1939, with war imminent, he decided to volunteer for the army. Being small and light he was selected for the Tank Regiment and he went to Catterick, in North Yorkshire, to train as a driver. When war broke out in September his unit went over to France as part of the British Expeditionary Force, but Neville was still not 18 and therefore could not serve overseas. So having qualified, he became an instructor, teaching others the tricky art of driving a tank.

He also learned to drive a car, and it was army policy to employ tank drivers as chauffeurs for staff cars, even though it required a totally different set of skills. On one occasion he had to drive an officer to the Rolls-Royce factory in Derby, and as Kirk Ireton was only a few miles away, the officer said he would not be required for the afternoon and could go home and see his family. However, when he rolled up outside his house in a very posh car, his mother's reaction was to ask if he had stolen it, and she took some persuading that he had not!

Neville spent the next four years as an instructor and driver, and found army life generally enjoyable. He particularly liked sport, especially football, hockey and cross-country running. However, in April 1944 he had his first experience of the horror of war. He was ordered to drive a senior officer to a secret location in the Dorset coast, where an exercise in preparation for the forthcoming D-Day landings was to be carried out. The idea was that a large force of American troops would make a landing from the sea as if they were an invasion force. All civilians had been vacated from the area, and to make it more realistic, live ammunition would be used to prepare the troops for the experience of real gunfire, but fired over their heads.

What happened next was as horrific as it was unexpected. All hell was suddenly let loose as a hail of shells rained down on the landing craft, pitching hundreds of men into the water where, laden with heavy kit and equipment, many drowned. Others had their arms and

Neville Dean took part in Operation Tiger, a joint US-UK training exercise in preparation for D-Day. It went disastrously wrong and many troops were killed. A Sherman tank stands today at Slapton Sands as a memorial to those who died.

legs blown off. The horrified observers, including the officer whom Neville had chauffeured, realised that the firing was coming from the sea. In fact it was a squadron of German E-Boats, fast armed patrol boats, that had stumbled accidentally on the landing craft and opened fire. Of the two warships that should have been protecting them, one was unserviceable and the other was in completely the wrong place. The E-Boats were finally driven off, but not before 946 American soldiers had needlessly lost their lives.

This calamity had taken place off Slapton Sands, and it did not become public knowledge until many years after the war. It was hushed up for fear of upsetting public morale, and Neville was sworn to secrecy for the rest of his life. It was only when he saw a television programme about it just a few years ago that he realised it was no longer classified information.

A few weeks later it was Neville's turn to be under enemy fire when, on 6 June, D-Day, he sailed from Gosport on a tank landing craft (LCT) and headed for Sword Beach. However, there was such a vast armada of ships on the approaches to the beach that they had to turn around, return to England, sail round the Isle of Wight and cross back over that night. This action could well have saved his life, for by the time they arrived the beach had been captured.

Over the next few months the Allies, despite fierce resistance, inexorably pushed the Germans back into their homeland. But they were not the only enemy that winter; the other was the bitterly cold weather, and in the Ardennes, where the temperature was twenty degrees below zero, they had to resort to any means they could to keep warm. When Neville and his crew came across an unoccupied house, they broke up everything that was made of wood to make a fire and keep warm.

On another occasion they were billeted in a farmhouse in which the animals lived on the ground floor and the people lived above them. Needing to relieve himself during the night, Neville accidentally fell over a cow and sprained his ankle. The next day he reported sick, and when asked by the medical officer how he had been injured, he gave the reason, but the officer thought he was lying and put him on a charge!

At Arnhem they watched the paratroops coming down as part of the ill-fated Operation Market Garden, an attempt to force an entry into Germany via Holland by capturing the bridges over the Rhine, which had it succeeded, would have considerably shortened the war. However, it failed, and the people of the Netherlands suffered terribly as the Germans cut off their food supplies.

Finally, they crossed the Rhine on pontoon bridges, but that was not without incident as one section of bridge became detached and floated off downstream carrying a tank! Now they were fighting their way to the heart of Germany, and in a last desperate attempt to undermine their morale the Germans dropped leaflets saying "Tommy go home. Your wives and sweethearts are fraternising with the Americans!" There may have been an element of truth in this, as many illicit relationships with American soldiers did take place, but it did not have the effect of causing the British to desert en masse and head back to England! Neville's unit ended up in Hanover, where

*The bridge at Nijmegen in the aftermath of Operation Market Garden,
September 1944.*

they witnessed round-the-clock bombing by the RAF and the US Air
Force, and where the noise of explosions was relentless.

The end of the war on 8 May found them in Holland, and Neville
recalls the ecstatic reception they received as they drove through
Amsterdam. Joyful civilians swarmed over the tanks, handing out
flowers to the liberating troops, their five year nightmare of German
occupation now over. However, there were now fresh problems.
Germany was awash with refugees, displaced people who had been
brought in as slave workers as well as Germans who were fleeing
from the advancing Russians. Many refused to admit to being
German, terrified of being sent back east to face the often barbaric
soldiers of the Red Army who were taking a terrible revenge for the
invasion of their country. Somehow, the occupying British had to try
to keep order in this chaos.

Later Neville was stationed in Paris, where one of his jobs was to
drive a staff car to Germany every fortnight. He experienced the
novelty of driving along motorways, which the Germans called
'Autobahnen'. No such high speed roads existed in Britain at the time,
and in fact it would be another fourteen years before M1 opened. On
one occasion they discovered a bombed car factory, and had great fun
racing brand new cars around a track!

Neville was demobbed in 1946, and returned to his trade as a bricklayer, though later he studied and became a buildings inspector. His only injury was caused when a shell exploded on the flail of a tank he was driving.(The flail was a device for exploding mines). The bang caused permanent deafness in his right ear.

For Neville the war years were a mixture of good and bad. He enjoyed teaching men how to drive a tank, and he enjoyed the sport; but the horrific memories of Slapton Sands and Belsen will never leave him.

Chris Hickinson

Infantryman, South Staffordshire Regiment

Chris worked in the lead mines in the Derbyshire village of Eyam (famous for the heroic decision of its inhabitants in 1665, when the plague broke out in the village, to seal themselves off and prevent it from spreading, thereby sacrificing two thirds of its population), until on 1 April 1943, at the age of eighteen, he was called up into the army. He did his basic training with the Sherwood Foresters, then was transferred to the South Staffordshire Regiment. Finally, he was sent to Inverary, in Scotland, for commando training in preparation for D Day.

Chris's active service was brief and bloody. Crossing the Channel to Gold Beach on 8 June 1944 (D-Day + 2), his unit went up the line and took over from the Royal Ulster Rifles on the outskirts of Caen. German resistance here was fierce, and there were many casualties. The town was being razed to the ground by a combination of heavy shelling and bombing by the RAF. Advancing on the town, Chris was horrified to see his comrades falling all around him. Corporal Parsons dropped dead on his left, Connor on his right. This was the last time he saw Bill Alcock, his pal from the start of training, and Frank Crackles, who lost an arm. That evening, under cover of darkness, they dragged all the dead back behind the lines. Chris looked enviously at their peaceful faces; they were now free from the hell raging all round them, whereas he would have to face the enemy again in a few hours' time. The attack the next morning was a failure, and there were heavy casualties. Chris and another man, found shelter in an empty building until nightfall, when they were able to crawl back over the lines. They were about the only two to survive.

During the night they were ordered to go with an artillery officer to a farm in the middle of 'no man's land' to observe the Germans' positions. They hid in a barn, and when daylight came they could see the Germans through holes in the roof. That night they returned under cover of darkness, but a shell exploded very close by. The officer and several of the men were killed, and Chris was wounded in the back by shrapnel. He was taken on a stretcher to a field hospital.

Chris has no recollection of how long he stayed in that hospital, but when he recovered he and another soldier from the North Staffs (who was killed shortly afterwards in the same trench as Chris) were sent to join the King's Own Scottish Borderers at the Falaise Gap, another place of fierce resistance by the Germans, which held up the Allied advance by several weeks.

Later, they entered the Belgian town of Geel from which the Germans had recently fled. It was always dangerous to do this, as there was likely to be a rearguard who would launch an unexpected attack. Such was the case on this occasion. Suddenly a hand grenade thrown from an upper window exploded right in front of Chris. He was severely wounded in the head, and was rushed to a field hospital and thence to an army hospital in Brussels. From there he was flown back to England and put on a hospital train to Nottingham. Finally he arrived at the Royal Hospital in Chesterfield, and from there he was sent to convalesce in Middleton-by-Youlgreave.

He was able to cycle home to High Cliff, near Eyam, and he was still convalescing when the war ended. However, he had to wait a year before he was demobbed, and during this time he had several postings, including Otley, where he was a guard in a prisoner-of-war camp. Quite unexpectedly, and bizarrely, he was sent out to Egypt, where he was given light duties as a courier, and where by chance he met his cousin Harry Greenan.

Chris had a final spell in hospital, this time to have a cyst removed from his neck. On being discharged from the hospital, he was surprised to find his name on the list to return to England, and on the 23 July 1946 he put on his double-breasted pinstripe demob suit and trilby hat and returned to civilian life.

It is hardly surprising that in the years since the war Chris has never wanted to return to Normandy on veterans' visits. He had seen and experienced too much suffering to wish to be reminded of those terrible days.

Eric Williamson

Tank Gunner, Royal Scots Greys

When Eric Williams, a paint mixer from Derby, sat in front of his television watching the wedding of Prince Charles and Lady Diana Spencer in July 1981, it was not the sight of the radiant, blushing young bride that caught his interest, but the man who walked beside her arm in arm down the aisle of St Paul's Cathedral. For Eric could truly say of the bride's father, Viscount Althorp, "I knew that man personally."

Forty years earlier, Eric had been a gunner in a tank commanded by Captain Edward John Spencer, later the 8th Earl Spencer, Viscount Althorp and father of Diana, Princess of Wales. The two men came from opposite ends of the social spectrum, but in the cramped, claustrophobic interior of a tank, class differences were far less important than the absolute necessity for the crew to work together as a team, each dependent on the other, in order to survive.

Such was the informal camaraderie between the two men that during their off-duty hours, Eric, observing Captain Spencer writing a letter, would ask jokingly, "Are you writing to your girlfriend the princess again?" The princess in question was none other

Gunner Eric Williamson

Eric Williams and a pal, both sporting the capbadge of the Royal Scots Greys

than Elizabeth, daughter of King George VI and the future Queen, then a young girl in her teens and already attracting the attention of eligible young men, including Lord Spencer. However, she had by this time already made up her mind on the subject of her future husband: a handsome naval lieutenant by the name of Philip Mountbatten. How ironic that it would eventually be Spencer's daughter that married Elizabeth's son. And, as events turned out, how tragic.

When the D Day invasion was imminent, Eric was told he could have 48 hours leave, but he was not to go more than 25 miles from the base in Worthing. Eric had other ideas. Knowing he might never see his family again, he was determined to go home to Derby. Unfortunately, he did not have enough money for his train fare, so he approached the only man who might have any, his captain. "OK," said Spencer, "I'll lend you ten bob, but I must have it back by Monday. Daddy doesn't give me much of an allowance!" This was probably the first time Eric realised that not all aristocrats are rolling in money, and that they were as liable as anyone else to be dependent on stingy parents!

Eric was eighteen when he joined the army in July 1942. He trained as a tank gunner on Salisbury Plain but his progress was interrupted by an accident when he was taking part in an inter-squadron competition on the assault course. While vaulting a wooden bar he fell, and as he landed he slashed his hand on a piece of glass. The injury was serious, as the glass had cut the tendons of his index finger, and he had to have two operations. The medical report read, "Injury likely to interfere with future efficiency." However, it does not appear to have done so, as Eric was able to return to full active service for the rest of the war.

In fact, injuries seem to have been a feature of Eric's army life. Three days before D-Day he was practising with a newly-issued Sten Gun when a bullet got stuck halfway into the chamber. An officer snatched the gun off him and fired it, but the bullet exploded, and part of it went into Eric's neck. (Some of it is still there to this day!). He had to go to hospital, and by the time he had recovered, his unit had crossed to France.

Although he had no connections with Scotland, Eric was in the Royal Scots Greys, the last regiment in the British Army to go into battle on horseback when, in February 1940, they had used horses to quell Arab riots in Palestine. In 1941 they exchanged their horses for tanks, and had seen action at El Alamein and in Italy. Eric had, in fact been with the regiment in North Africa and Italy but had seen no action. On 7 June 1944 they had crossed to Normandy, and Eric joined them on the 22nd when he came out of hospital.

Eric was in a 'floating regiment', i.e. they plugged gaps in the line. This meant that they often had to move at short notice. Each tank crew was issued with a box of rations, and one member had to be duty cook. This job fell to Eric, and one day they had just obtained a chicken, which was cooking nicely when suddenly they were ordered to move immediately. Much to their dismay, the chicken had to be abandoned. Such are the hardships of war!

The interior of a tank was dark, often stiflingly hot and frequently full of smoke. Not surprisingly, it could cause claustrophobia, as happened one day when the radio operator suddenly shouted "Let me out. Let me out! I can't breathe!" The driver, a former London policeman, opened the hatch to let him out and then knocked him out cold with a single blow! When he came round he had recovered from his panic attack. Eric has never lost his fear of being trapped, and to this day always sleeps with the doors and curtains of his bedroom open.

During the bitter winter of 1944-45 the Allies drove the Germans back through France, Belgium and Holland, and on 25 March they crossed the Rhine into Germany. On 1 May, one week before VE Day, Eric's regiment arrived in Wismar, a country town on the Baltic. They had been anxious to get there before the Russians, who were rapidly advancing westward, and after a non-stop drive of seventy miles they arrived just eight hours before the Red Army. They were, in fact, the first British troops to make contact with the Soviets.

After the surrender of the Germans the regiment had to police the surrounding area and try to keep the peace among the newly-liberated slave labourers, mostly from eastern Europe, who were out to extract revenge after the brutal treatment they had received.

Eric was demobilised in February 1946 and returned to his job as a paint mixer in Derby. His first wife, Violet, whom he married the following September, died in 1963, and five years later he married his present wife, Irene. She said he sometimes feels emotional when he reflects on the war, reliving bad memories that never go away.

George Arthur Wilson

Gunner, Royal Artillery

George Wilson, who died in 1986, was the father of Margaret Tadman, from Ripley, the wife of Richard Tadman, who will feature twice in this book, first as a boy growing up in wartime Kent, and later as National Serviceman in the early 1950s. Margaret kindly furnished me with details of her father's war service.

George's story has much in common with that of Francis Elgar (q.v.), in that they both had to endure a long sea journey to the Far East. In late 1941 his unit, 278 Heavy Anti Aircraft Regiment, boarded HMT Strathallan, a luxury liner built to carry 1000 passengers but now having to accommodate 7000 troops. Eventually they arrived in Cape Town, where they stayed for four days while the ship refuelled and restocked with provisions. It was four days of sheer bliss after the cramped conditions of the Strathallan. On 6 September they sailed on to Bombay. Many other places were to follow (some to become only to familiar to us in a much more recent conflict): Basra, Bagdad, Kirkuk, Palestine, Africa (where they were joined by black soldiers from Bechuanaland, now Botswana), on to Italy and finally home.

Margaret tells of "one very special memory I should like to share of my dad's stay in Cape Town. The family with whom he was billeted

The troopship, HMT Strathallen, in which George Williamson travelled to the Far East in 1941

sent us back home in England every Christmas from 1941 to the end of rationing a linen bag containing mixed dried fruit, raisins, currents and candied peel – an absolute luxury in wartime England.

"My mother, like so many women during the war, worked so hard bringing up a young family, caring for my grandmother who lived with us, managing an allotment complete with chickens, and working in a day nursery. But life did have its lighter side. One day Mum was on a bus with my sister and me, and a passenger said "What lovely girls. Where's their dad?" "I only wish I knew" said my mum. "The villain!" said the irate passenger, putting money into her hand and getting off the bus before Mum could explain that letters were censored and she had no idea where he was!"

Military personnel were well fed and often had no idea how limited the food rations were for civilians. On one occasion he came home on leave and the next morning got up early and made himself some breakfast. Later he said to his wife "I've enjoyed my breakfast. That corned beef was lovely." Unknowingly he had eaten the family's meat ration for the rest of that week!

Gunner George Wilson,
278 H.A.A Battery,
Royal Artillery, 1939-45

Joe Holmes

Bombardier in the Royal Artillery

Joe Holmes can claim to be a true D-Day veteran, for in the early hours of 6 June 1944 he was among the first British troops to experience the terrifying ordeal of landing on the Normandy beaches, totally exposed to machine gun fire, mortar and aerial bombardment. He managed to survive, and with his anti-aircraft battery fought his way through France, Belgium, Holland and finally Germany.

In 1942, 18-year-old Joe, from the village of Tupton, near Chesterfield, (the village in which twelve people were killed when a German bomber, trying to escape from a pursuing fighter, dropped its load of bombs to gain speed) joined the army. He did his basic training in Perth, and was posted to the Royal Artillery to learn to use new and very 'hush hush' equipment called 'radiolocation', later known as 'radar', used by anti-aircraft gunners to locate enemy aircraft so that they could be accurately targeted.

He was then posted to Pembroke Dock, in South Wales. As German bombers rarely came that far west, there was very little action during the several months they were there, and they became part of this friendly community. Eventually came the order to move on, which caused consternation among those comrades who had formed romantic attachments!

His unit was sent to Teesside, where again there was little action, so they went south again to Hove, in Sussex, and it was here that Joe nearly lost his life, though not through enemy action. GL (Ground Location, or radar) personnel did not normally operate the AA guns, but were sometimes called upon to relieve regular gunners. In his inexperience, Joe was standing too close to the gun being fired as a white-hot shell case was ejected. A quick-thinking sergeant lunged forward to push him out of the way and in doing so severely burned his arm. He was rushed to hospital, but so severe was his injury that he had to be discharged from the army.

In most aspects of warfare the Germans were ruthlessly efficient, but in espionage they were generally hopelessly incompetent. Almost all the spies operating in Britain were caught, and many were 'turned', i.e. persuaded to send false signals to their German operators. In this way much disinformation about the Allied preparation for D-Day was fed to the Germans, who were thereby led to believe that the invasion force would be landing in the Pas de Calais rather than Normandy. Joe witnessed an example of their ineptitude when one day a civilian was spotted on a beach near Hove looking up the cliff through a pair of binoculars. As beaches were out of bounds, this naturally aroused suspicion and a squad of Coldstream Guardsmen went down to question him. He was, indeed, an enemy agent and was immediately arrested and imprisoned.

Soon Joe's unit was on the move again, first to Falmouth, in Cornwall, where it was again very quiet, then north to York. They were stationed at an RAF airfield, where they had to sleep in tents. One night a fierce gale blew several tents away, leaving the occupants rather exposed. Joe was lucky, however. His tent remained firmly in place and he slept soundly through it all. He managed to snatch 48 hours leave while at York, which enabled him to make a brief visit home, but he found it a bit disconcerting when the first thing his family said was "When are you going back?" Of course, he knew it did not mean he was unwelcome, merely that they wanted to know how short a time they were going to see him for.

Some time later the battery was disbanded and Joe was sent north to Dornoch, in Scotland. Here they joined 32 Battery of 103 Heavy Anti Aircraft (HAA) Regiment, a very experienced unit, and they underwent rigorous training in invasion tactics. Their job would be to land shortly after the initial assault and prepare gun and instrument positions. Even when practising it was necessary to be extremely careful to avoid tragic accidents, as happened during a mine-laying exercise when two sergeants were badly injured after a detonator had gone off in their faces. One was blinded.

Finally, the training over, it was time to head back down south to Horsham, in Sussex, where the invasion force was being assembled. Every lane in the area was lined with guns, tanks and military vehicles of every kind.

The landing craft on which they were to cross the channel was designed to carry tanks and was known as the LCT. It was not lacking in comforts, having bunks below deck, showers, and a galley serving food that was considerably superior to army fare. Before they put to sea, the Master at Arms told Joe and his pal Alf Beard that as they were artillery trained they were to man the 20mm Oerlikon anti-aircraft gun in the event of an attack. This was a totally unfamiliar weapon to them, and the two minutes instruction they received left them very nervous about their ability to defend the ship. Luckily, they did not have to.

They set off, but after a few hours turned round and came back . They were not told why, but assumed it was a dummy run. That night they set off again, and this time it was the real thing. Joe has written a vivid account of the landing as part of an unpublished story of his wartime service called 'D of E to C of E', which I shall now quote in full.

"We were amazed to find ourselves in a great armada, with craft of all shapes and sizes moving in the same direction. Excitedly, we could plainly discern the skyline and knew that this was the real thing. We became aware that our neighbour, a huge battleship whose 15-inch guns were firing salvoes inland. This was HMS Warspite.

"As we approached the coast the sound of gunfire and bombing became more intense. Eventually the ship hove to and dropped anchor. We were ordered down to the hold amid the assembled guns and vehicles. The two huge doors were swung open and a 'Rhino' ferry joined up to the entrance. This strange but simple-looking contraption was, in effect, a large raft of steel plates, riding on buoyancy tanks and steered by a traditional ship's wheel. The helmsman was a Sapper of the Royal Engineers, who appeared to be in charge. He must have been the most junior rank ever to have been in command! Several jeeps and other light vehicles were embarked and secured to the ferry Then we proceeded steadily to the beach, which was about three quarters of a mile away.

"There was a very uncomfortable feeling of exposure about this journey, and we all felt that everything would be better when we arrived. Eventually we left the Rhino grinding on the beach and we went ashore. The first sight we saw was an amputated leg still wearing

Vehicles and equipment transfer from a landing craft to a 'Rhino' ferry prior to a beach landing.

a sock and army boot. Just away from the water's edge a small party of medics were urgently treating some casualties, who appeared to be in a pretty bad way. A young, obviously overwrought RAMC officer shouted to me that I could not land there. I did not reply and simply moved on.

"There was a lot of noise and shouting. A Naval officer wearing khaki battledress beckoned us forward with the utmost urgency. We started to run up the beach past a jeep that looked as if it had been trodden on by a gigantic foot. The crew were slumped in their seats, very obviously dead. There were cries of "Take cover!" as an enemy fighter swooped over the beach firing its machine guns. We dived into some sparse grass which was growing in the sand dune. There were some hastily-dug slit trenches, which were still occupied. Sadly, these lads had no further use for them.

"Our party was hurriedly regrouped and heads counted. Fortunately nobody was missing. Two RAF airmen who had been in charge of the barrage balloon fastened astern on the LCT had temporarily anchored it nearby and had no idea what to do next, so I said "Stick with us." They were in blue battledress but without the regulation collar and tie. Suddenly a Flight Lieutenant appeared and gave them an outsize 'rocket' for being improperly dressed!

" We were now ordered to move forward, and bearing an assortment of ·303 ammunition bandoliers, Bren gun magazines, wire cutters, shovels and scrimming tape ,we moved on in file with weapons at the ready. On the way through the village of Lion-sur-Mer we came to a crossroads, where a solitary military policeman was directing traffic. He looked very vulnerable and lonely, and with good reason, for we later found out he was the third to occupy that position, his predecessors having fallen victim to snipers.

"On the outskirts of the village, as we approached the meadow which was our intended destination, we were subjected to bursts of sub machine-gun fire. No-one needed to order "Take cover!" because we all dived into the nearest ditch. There being no repetition, we cautiously climbed out and moved forward. On arriving at our destination, we found a Centaur self-propelled field gun, a 75 mm I think, busily engaging an unseen target. There was also a Bofors LAA (light anti-aircraft) mounted on a 15 hundredweight truck chassis. Its detachment had obviously been in action.

"We had positioned ourselves by a hedge and were hurriedly digging personal slit trenches, two men to a trench. I shared mine with Lance Bombardier Joe Stockley. There was a sustained rattle of automatic gunfire as a German fighter plane flew over, its tail on fire. Suddenly the Bofors crew trained their gun on the church steeple and pumped five rounds in the direction of a small aperture. This action was supported by a full magazine burst from our Bren gun, manned by our Battery Sergeant Major and a sergeant. Then a group of Royal Marine Commandos entered the church and flushed out several snipers, one of whom was a woman.

"Joe Stockley and I mounted our PIAT (Projector Infantry Anti-Tank), a heavy and clumsy weapon but our sole defence against enemy armour. Fortunately, nothing happened and after a while we were recalled. However, we had little time to rest as a party of us were detailed to assist a Pioneer Corps detachment to lay a smoke screen. After hurried instruction we laid out a line of canisters, which emitted a thick, pungent, unpleasant-smelling smoke. Having completed the task we returned to our position. We never did discover what we were protecting by the smoke screen.

"As we sat in our slit trenches a sergeant passed us each a small can of spam and a packet of hard tack biscuits. We brewed tea from our Oxo-tin-sized packets of 'compo' tea which was a mixture of tea leaves, sugar and powdered milk. The water came from our bottles and was heated by a 'Tommy cooker', a small hexamine tablet resting on a tiny container which, when ignited, burned fiercely for about five minutes. Calls of nature were answered furtively and as quickly as possible, using whatever cover could be found.

"It was now late evening and there appeared to be a general lessening of the noise of warfare. As the dusk deepened, word was passed along the line of slit trenches for one occupant of each to stay on watch whilst the other attempted to sleep. After an hour or so the sleeping one would be awakened and would take his turn on watch. I remember being in a sitting position at the bottom of the trench, wrapped in my one blanket and covered with my ground sheet. Strangely enough, I slept until it was my turn to take watch."

So ended Joe's first day on enemy soil. The following day they set up their anti-aircraft guns on Ouistreham marshes. This was a most unhealthy place, and they were plagued by malarial mosquitoes. They attempted to dig slit trenches but were unable to do so because the water table was too high. They would strike water at a spade's depth. They had to improvise shelters with tarpaulins draped from trucks.

It was now that they shot down their first two enemy aircraft. One crashed nearby and they went to inspect it. It was a JU88 bomber. The crew were all dead, all badly burned. Later they saw an American Marauder bomber which the crew had abandoned, as they could see by the parachutes. With nobody at the controls it flew crazily in all directions, including theirs briefly, before crashing into the sea. They also saw the first 'doodle bugs', the V1 flying bombs that were starting to be launched on London, as well as on Antwerp and Brussels.

The town of Caen, which Montgomery had hoped to capture on D-Day, became a centre of fierce, stubborn German resistance over the next few weeks, and to try to bring this to an end the RAF launched a thousand bomber raid on it. Inevitably, many civilians would be killed as well as enemy troops. Joe witnessed this awesome armada as wave after wave of bombers passed overhead. The anti-aircraft guns were putting up a barrage of flak, and he saw one Lancaster burst into flames and plummet to the ground.

103 HAA was a very effective unit, and its commanding officer was later awarded the OBE for successful defence of the beachhead and surrounding areas. Their first casualty was not through enemy action but because of a 'short burst', where a shell exploded immediately after leaving the barrel, a situation dreaded by all gun crews. A sergeant caught the full force of the shrapnel and was so severely wounded that he never returned from hospital. Another casualty of so-called 'friendly fire' was a man who was accidentally shot by a fellow soldier fooling around with a Sten gun. He pointed it at his friend in jest and accidentally pulled the trigger, fatally wounding him. The offender was given 180 days Field Punishment, which involved the unpleasant task of battlefield clearance and burying the dead.

After several weeks of living on hard tack they received a special treat: white bread, the first they had eaten since leaving England. They were also given tins of steak and kidney pudding, canned peaches, and chocolate, as well as luxuries such as cigarettes and toilet paper! Another treat was going swimming at Luc-sur-Mer. This gave them the chance to get clean after several weeks without washing facilities.

As they advanced through Northern France they passed through newly-liberated towns where some occupants waved and cheered but others stood in sullen silence, resentful of the damage done to their town. They crossed into Belgium passing through Ypres and the Menin Gate, scenes of mass slaughter in the First World War, marked by thousands of crosses.

Coming into Holland, a mishap occurred when the '584' radar set slid off the lorry and into a shell hole beside the road, which was little more than a cart track. The towing vehicle was unhitched and driven away with the rest of the troop, leaving Joe and Ted Hughes (not the poet!) to guard this highly secret piece of equipment all night in the bitter cold, huddled in their greatcoats and leather jerkins. The recovery truck arrived next morning, much to their relief, and winched the '584' back onto the road, though not without nearly

The 584 Mobile Radar equipment, typical of the one that Joe Holmes encountered in a ditch during the advance into Holland in 1944

decapitating an NCO when one of the wire ropes snapped.

In this freezing weather they were living in tents, and keeping warm was top priority. They acquired some wood-burning stoves which they placed at the entrance to the tents, using metal sheets to shield the canvas. In this way they made themselves reasonably comfortable, although they were plagued with mice, who also found this an agreeable billet!

On Christmas Day the time-honoured army tradition of role-reversal was observed, where the officers served dinner to the men. Joe, being the youngest member, was 'orderly officer' for the day. His duties included inspecting the guard and asking if there were any complaints. There were none, as the cooks had produces a first-class meal which included rum and lager. However, their celebrations were rudely interrupted by the Luftwaffe, but there were no casualties.

Joe was promoted to acting Lance Bombardier (Lance Corporal) early in the new year. The Luftwaffe returned in strength and attacked airfields all over Holland, Belgium and Northern France. Joe's unit was in constant action, and shot down several aircraft. It was a last desperate effort by the enemy to turn the tide of the war, but their losses were so severe that they never returned to an attacking role.

Finally they reached the Rhine and crossed into Germany. They were under strict orders not to fraternise with the Germans, but Joe found himself in an embarrassing situation one day when his truck developed a puncture. As he and his mate Ken struggled to get the wheel off, a ten-year-old German boy, unbidden, came up and took over the job. He expertly changed the wheel in front of the shamefaced Joe and Ken, as well as other amused onlookers! When the job was finished they surreptitiously slipped him a bar of chocolate and sent him on his way.

At Osnabruck they occupied a military airfield. When a squadron of German aircraft came into view they manned the guns in readiness, but instead of launching an attack the aircraft landed and the pilots climbed out and surrendered, a clear sign that the war was coming to an end.

On 7 May, the day before VE Day, it was announced that the Germans were about to surrender, but for some reason they were not allowed to celebrate, and it was just a normal day. They knew that although the war in Europe was over the fighting in the Far East was set to go on for possibly another two years, and that rather than being sent home they might well be shipped off to Burma. However, the dropping of the atomic bombs in August made that unnecessary.

The war may have been over, but it would be another two years before Joe went home for good. Like many of the other soldiers in this book, he found himself having to try to police the lawless bands of Displaced Persons, slave labourers from Poland and Russia. Travelling round the country, Joe saw for himself the terrible destruction of cities such as Hamburg.

The demob programme created vacancies for promotion, and Joe received a second stripe to make him a Bombardier. He acquired a dog, Stag, which he had to pass on to another man when his turn came in May 1947.

Joe liked the army, and they obviously liked him, because he was asked by his colonel to consider applying for a commission. However, his mother firmly put the lid on that idea. She had worried about her son for five years, and she was not going to see him risking his life any longer!

So it was back to Civvy Street and his old job at Sheepbridge Works, but like many returning servicemen he found it hard to adjust. Those who had avoided military service were now well established, and Joe decided to move on. He gained accountancy qualifications and went to work for British Steel.

Looking back on his wartime experiences, Joe has many memories he would rather forget, but also a lot of good times, and he felt his life was richer for the experience.

Francis Elgar

Captain in the Somerset Light Infantry

Of all the war zones to which a soldier could be sent in the Second World War, arguably the worst was the Far East. Here he faced not only a ferocious, fanatical enemy for whom the rules of the Geneva Convention meant nothing, surrender was unthinkable and whose treatment of enemy prisoners was inhuman and barbaric, but he often had to fight in steamy, impenetrable jungles where leeches were as much an enemy as the Japanese and where he was as likely to die from malaria as from enemy action. Thousands of miles away on the far side of the world, he could never get home on leave and would be away from his family for several years. To the men of the 14th Army in India and Burma it seemed as if their homeland had turned its back on them Indeed, they called themselves the 'Forgotten Fourteenth'.

It was to the Far East that Francis Elgar was sent in 1942. Born in Frome, Somerset, in 1915, he went to grammar school and then to Bristol University, where he studied chemistry and also met his future wife, Margaret. Graduating in 1936, he became a teacher, and later a housemaster, at the London Orphan School in Watford. When it became obvious that he would be called up for war service he married Margaret on 9 April 1940, the day after his twenty-fifth birthday.

On 13 June he enlisted in the Chemical Warfare branch of the Royal Engineers at Barton Stacey. Although the army was renowned for posting men to trades for which they were totally unsuitable, on this occasion, Francis having a chemistry degree, they managed to get a round peg in a round hole.. He later wrote, "In that baking summer I did my infantry training – drill, marching, digging World War One trenches in the chalk and rubble of Salisbury Plain, rifle shooting, then on to Bangalore Torpedoes, petrol bombs, etc, and I earned my proficiency pay by running 100 yards carrying a 120 pound poison gas cylinder on my shoulder!"

Lance Corporal Francis Elgar, pictured in training at Barton Stacey Camp in 1940 ...

Between January and March 1941, Francis did his officer training in "frozen Dunbar, where my abiding memory was having to eat my porridge with salt instead of sugar", and on completion was commissioned in the Somerset Light Infantry. He spent the next year training in East Anglia, where he learned to ride a motor bike and found it difficult as an umpire to persuade members of the Home Guard that they were 'dead' and had to lie down during exercises! On one occasion he had to take his platoon to a village "where members of the chapel were very kind to us and gave us their harvest festival produce, resulting in most of the platoon becoming Methodists!"

Life became more serious when, in 1942, Francis learned that his battalion was being posted to the Far East. By now Japan had entered the war and its army had advanced at frightening speed down the Malay Peninsula and captured Singapore. There was a real risk that the whole of the Far East, including India, the jewel in the imperial crown, would fall under Japanese rule, so thousands of British troops were being sent to strengthen their defences.

On 6th May 1942 the battalion boarded the MV Athlone Castle, a newly-built liner converted to a troopship. Francis wrote a detailed 34-page account of this voyage, and his subsequent life in India, to

.. and in October 1941, as Lieutenant Elgar, Somerset Light Infantry

Margaret in August of that year, which I have summarised and quoted extensively in the following pages.

The ship sailed from Liverpool, which made parting particularly difficult for Francis, because not only had Margaret recently given birth to Joy, their first child, but he had spent his embarkation leave with her family, who lived very near the Mersey, and the ship passed within yards of their home. He wrote, "As we moved away, no scenery had ever been so lovely or so infinitely desirable. How I envied the crews of the tugs and harbour boats. They could go home to their wives and families when they had finished work, while I was to go voyaging dangerously to an unknown destination and had no idea at all when I'd see you and Joy again."

Conditions were extremely cramped on the ship, which was carrying eight times the number for which it was designed. Francis was lucky to share a cabin with just four officers. Others were crowded into whatever open spaces were available, with between forty and a hundred officers in each. The former First Class lounge was christened the Altmark, (the German ship which had rescued 299 sailors from ships that had been sunk by the battleship Graf Spee, and where they had been held in extremely cramped conditions until rescued by HMS Cossack in February 1940). Here they slept in bunks five tiers high, with no hot water and cold water strictly rationed. The lower ranks slept in hammocks in the bowels of the ship, though as the climate grew warmer they took to sleeping on the deck, glad to escape the stifling heat down below.

On 6 June they arrived in Cape Town, and were hugely impressed by the sight of Table Mountain. Here they were able to disembark and enjoy a few days' freedom after the cramped conditions of the ship. They also enjoyed the generous South African hospitality. Many people took them into their homes and entertained them. With no blackout, no rationing, and no air raids, it was a wonderfully refreshing change from drab wartime Britain. They were thrilled to see the giant 'Queen Mary' steaming into port, travelling unescorted as she was too fast for the U-boats, and was rumoured to contain 21,000 troops! To keep the men fit they were sent on a five-mile route march, during which it poured in torrents, and some had no dry clothes to change into when they got back to the ship.

Five days later, the ship now provisioned and refuelled, the voyage continued. The sea was calm, but when they reached the Cape of Good Hope it became very rough indeed. Finally, on 2 July, two months and fourteen thousand miles after leaving Liverpool, they arrived in Bombay. Francis was not impressed. "Just an example of the ugliness which is obtained by trying to anglicise the East," he commented. The following day they set off on the fifteen hundred mile journey to their final destination, the town of Gandai. At Rawlpindi they had to change and wait twelve hours for the onward train, which was crowded and terribly hot. On the previous train there had been fans to keep them cool, but on this one there were none. They eventually came to a river, but the bridge was down and they had to get out and wade across to board a waiting train on the other side.

Finally, on 10 July, they reached Gandai. They were now no longer in British India but in Wiziristan, a land of lawless, hostile tribesmen which, after partition in 1947, became part of Pakistan. To reach the camp they had to travel along a dangerous road where they were highly likely to be ambushed. It was closed to traffic except on RODs (Road Open Days), when it would be guarded along its length by troops and vehicles travelled in convoys. The road rose from a thousand to five thousand feet and was described by Francis as "an engineering masterpiece, built in 1920 to open up Wiziristan to civilisation (some hope!)" In places it was a series of hairpin bends dug out of the mountain side. The camp was a huge collection of building with mud and stone walls and tent roofs, surrounded by dry-stone walls and barbed wire. Their job was to guard the road on RODs, which meant positioning themselves at various points along the road until the last vehicle had gone by.

One night the camp was attacked by tribesmen. Francis wrote, "Bullets suddenly started whistling past all around me, and in a flash I was flat on the ground. Bullets coming over you are strange – you actually don't heat them until they've passed, although it sounds as if it suddenly starts whistling a few yards in front of you, then whines away into the distance a few yards behind you for several seconds." The attackers were beaten back and disappeared into the night.

One morning Francis woke up with violent diarrhoea. "I was diagnosed with dysentery and spent three frightful days in a field ambulance, where I lived in a pigsty and was completely neglected – no food, no treatment, not even water was given to me, except when my bearer came to see me and I sent him for something. Then one morning I dressed and sat in the front of an ambulance and went to Razmah Hospital 28 miles away, with a heavy escort of armoured cars and troop-carrying vehicles. It was a non-ROD day but luckily we were not attacked. My treatment at Razmah was simply starvation for ten days and three doses of salts, which was all I needed."

Several weeks later, now fully recovered, Francis was posted to Delhi and was made Battalion Intelligence Officer. His worst job was internal security, which meant dealing with riots and keeping order during civil disturbances. Luckily his battalion was never called out. The nearest they got was a boring day spent in New Delhi Police Station, when trouble was expected but never materialised.

The letter ceases at this point. What happened to the rest is not known, and the only other available information on Francis' service is a series of brief and rather cryptic notes which he no doubt intended to write up sometime. Unfortunately, he never did, and in April 2012 he passed away, aged 96. A few weeks earlier I had made contact with Judith, his younger daughter, and she kindly loaned me his letters, notes and photographs, but I could not talk to Francis himself as he was in hospital. Sadly, I never did get to meet him. It would have been fascinating to talk to him.

I can, therefore, only try to piece together the rest of his story from his notes. After Delhi he had various postings throughout India, including the Punjab, Calcutta and Peshawar. He does not seem to have come into contact with the Japanese until February 1945, when he flew to Burma. His notes read as follows:

March 1945: Joined 2nd Welch Regiment.

April 1945: Advancing south in Burma.

July – August 1945: Fighting on Maurchi Road. Went over bridge into river with truck.

September 1945: Rangoon. Tent caught fire. Flag march in Shan States. Presented with ceremonial sword by Myosa of Ye-Negan, local ruler.

October 1945: Voyage home from Rangoon.

It would seem that most of Francis' service in the Far East was spent keeping the peace in India, with only the last few months fighting the Japanese in Burma, but no doubt it was a necessary job in view of the rising tide of rebellion against British rule at the time, which culminated in the granting of independence in 1947.

Francis ended the war as a company commander with the rank of captain. After demobilisation he took a post at Chesterfield Boys' Grammar School, where he taught science until retirement in 1975. He and Margaret had a second daughter, Judith, in 1946. He had three grandchildren and six great-grandchildren.

Jean Sealey

Signals Officer at Bletchley Park

Jean Sealey, from Dunstable, wanted to join the armed forces but did not find it easy. First she tried the WRNS, but they only wanted people with relations who had served in the Navy; then she tried the WAAF, but they were only looking for women to do secretarial work, and as she was already a secretary for a manager at AC Spark Plugs she wanted something different; finally, she tried the ATS (Auxiliary Territorial Service, the women's army), and following an interview deep underground in a building in Whitehall she was accepted for intelligence work.

After three weeks basic training (which should have been six but was shortened as they urgently needed personnel) she was sent to a place in Bedfordshire which remained top secret until many years after the war but is now world famous: Bletchley Park.

Officially known as the Government Code and Cypher School (GC and CS), it recruited from Oxford, Cambridge and other top universities some of the most brilliant minds in the country – linguists, chess champions, mathematicians, and crossword solvers, to decrypt the cyphers and codes used by the Germans on their Enigma and Lorenzo machines. The codes were virtually unbreakable, and it was only after hundreds of hours of trial-and-error by the code breakers and some sloppy German operator behaviour that the breakthrough finally came. As a result, the allies were able to win the Battle of the Atlantic by knowing where the U-boats were located, defeat Rommel in North Africa and ensure that the main force of the German army was in the wrong place (i.e. the Pas de Calais, not Normandy) to meet the invading allies on D-Day in June 1944. The work done at Bletchley Park was considered to have shortened the war by two to four years. Churchill called it "The goose that laid the golden egg but never cackled."

Jean's work was not with Enigma, but another code-breaking

One of the preserved buildings at Bletchley Park, where Jean Sealey spent 'her war'

machine called Lorenz, which intercepted messages between the German high command and the field commanders. Her job was to check radio signals and pass them on for further decoding. She never knew what they said. So tight was the security at Bletchley that few people knew what anyone else was doing, and in their social time they never talked about their work. Neither could they talk about it to their friends or family, as they were bound by the Official Secrets Act for life. However, during the 1970s information on the work done there came into the public domain, although the ban was never officially lifted. Many of its workers went to their graves without revealing their involvement there.

Work went on round the clock in eight-hour shifts, with a meal break half way through. Over 12,000 people worked there at some time during the war, 80% of them women. Life at Bletchley was relatively comfortable, even though they worked in wooden huts rather than in the grand Victorian Gothic house. They were adequately fed compared with the civilian population (although she does recall having mashed potatoes on toast in one of her billets!), and there were good recreational facilities. Since there were many highly educated people around, a great deal of intellectual activity

Not all work ... Jean Sealey in a Bletchley Park amateur production of 'Berkeley Square in 1943

took place, and the drama productions, in which Jean was involved, were of a high standard. "It was", she said, "my university. I mixed with many nationalities: Polish, Free French, and the glamorous Americans!"

So tight was the security that the Germans never found out what went on at Bletchley, so consequently it was never bombed, although one stray bomb did land on one of the huts when it was under construction. In fact Jean's only experience of bombing was on a weekend visit to London when she heard a V1 coming over and then exploding. It made her aware of the hardships of people living in London, and what an 'easy' war she was having by comparison.

Jean was at Bletchley Park for two and a half years, and was discharged to get married at the end of the war. Her husband, a former Halifax bomber pilot, trained as a maths teacher and later worked with special needs children. They finally settled in Belper, where Jean, now a widow of 91, still lives in the family home.

Apart from its role in providing information of incalculable value to the war effort, Bletchley Park is also famous as the birthplace of the computer. Thanks to the work of the brilliant Alan Turing, "the father of computer science", the world's first programmable digital electronic computer was invented. Jean saw him several times but never got to speak to him.

The Oldridge Brothers

Ratings in the Royal Navy

To be accepted for service in the Royal Navy, it was usually necessary to have a nautical background. Bob and Alf Oldridge, from Barton-on-Humber in Lincolnshire, were the sons and grandsons, not of seafarers, but of barge skippers on the River Humber. However, their father had served on minesweepers during the First World War, so it was natural that when their turn came to serve their country, they would join the Royal Navy .

Bob was the elder of the two. Born in 1923, he joined up in 1941. After eleven weeks' basic training at Devonport, he went to a bomb disposal school in Cumbria (on the site of the present Sellafield Nuclear Power Station) for eight months, then returned to Devonport for a six-month course that qualified him as a torpedoman.

He was posted to HMS Richmond, an American lend-lease destroyer, and for the next two and a half years was on convoy escort duty in the North Atlantic. Based at Halifax, Nova Scotia, they would meet the convoys of merchant ships from Britain at the half-way point and escort them to St John's Newfoundland, Halifax, Boston or New York, attempting to protect them from marauding German U-boats which were inflicting devastating losses on the ships bringing vital war supplies to Britain. Richmond claimed three kills, two with depth charges and one which they rammed. However, it was the presence of warships that deterred the U-boats from getting within range of their targets to fire their torpedoes.

Sadly, Bob saw many ships torpedoed, and if it was safe to stop they would try to save the survivors, lowering rope netting over the side for them to climb up, if they were able to. More often than not, however, they had to keep going and leave the survivors to their fate, or the whole convoy would be put in danger. They had to be especially careful as they entered harbour, as this was where the enemy would often lie in wait to attack.

Bob Oldridge, Cath his wife, and Alf Oldridge in 1946

The weather was, in some ways, a worse enemy than the Germans. Hurricane-force winds and mountainous seas made life very uncomfortable on board these small ships, although Bob only once suffered a bout of seasickness. This was after a night on the beer, followed by a drink of greasy hot chocolate! In time-honoured Naval tradition, each man received a daily issue of rum, though only the petty officers drank it neat. The ratings had theirs watered down 'three-on-one'. i.e. three parts water to one part rum, though on special occasions this became two-on-one. No doubt the rum helped to keep out the cold when, as often happened, the temperature dropped to twenty degrees below zero. Salt water stuck to the rails, which had to be constantly de-iced with hammers.

Although Bob never got home during this time, he did get shore leave. He once had fourteen days, and a Canadian shipmate kindly invited him to his home in Ontario, where he was very hospitably treated. He enjoyed dancing, but did not find the Canadian girls very friendly; they seemed to prefer the local boys. He had a wonderful time in New York, where in contrast to blacked-out Britain everything was brilliantly lit up at night. At the YMCA he could get tickets to the dance halls, and has a particularly fond memory of the Policeman's Ball.

Later in the war, Bob was posted to HMS Witch, carrying out experimental work in Rosyth, testing paravanes for blowing up mines. These were a kind of towed underwater 'gliders'. The towing cable would cut the cable anchoring the mine, thus causing it to rise to the surface, where it could be blown up by gunfire. They also developed countermeasures against 'acoustic fish', devices attached to torpedoes that picked up the sound of a ship, enabling the torpedo to home in on it. They countered this by using rattler bars to simulate the sound of a ship and send the torpedoes in the wrong direction.

After demobilisation Bob returned to his trade as a bricklayer and later worked for a cement company in Castleton, Derbyshire.

Alf followed his older brother into the Navy in 1943 when he reached the age of 18. Since leaving school at 14 he had led an active life as a member of the Home Guard, the Air Training Corps and the St John Ambulance Brigade.

His first billet was the former Butlins Holiday Camp at Skegness, renamed HMS Royal Arthur. (It is one of the Navy's idiosyncratic traditions that all shore establishments are named as if they are ships!). He then went to Ayr to train as a telegraphist, where he had to reach 21 words a minute, after which he went to the signals school at Chatham.

Alf's first operational posting was not to sea but to Dover Castle, under which a network of caves housed the Navy's communication system. Though land based, he was by no means safe, as they were frequently shelled by enemy ships. On one occasion he was making his way to the NAAFI when a shell made

Alf Oldridge enjoying time off with friends in Australia, 1945

Alf Oldridge's class photograph in HMS Royal Arthur in 1943. Alf is in the second row 'somewhere in the middle'

a direct hit on the building. Two minutes later he would have been inside it! Alf was there receiving messages all through D-Day, and he could clearly see the vast armada of warships and landing craft making their way across the Channel. He also saw the first V1 flying bombs, one of thousands that would be launched on England during the next few months.

Alf's only war wound was not as a result of enemy action but of playing football! He injured his cartilage and had to spend a few weeks in Chatham Hospital. It was early in 1945 that he made his first sea voyage, but that was only in a paddle steamer to Harwich! However, his next voyage was a little longer – to Sydney, Australia. There he was posted first to a Naval base on Sydney Racetrack and then to a transmitting station near Canberra.

The war in Europe came to an end in May 1945, but Japan was far from defeated, and preparations were being made to continue the war in the Far East. However, the dropping of the atomic bombs on the cities of Hiroshima and Nagasaki brought about the Japanese surrender much sooner than expected.

Alf was demobbed in June 1946, and like his brother he went to work for the cement company in Castleton. However, his life took an unexpected turn in 1956 when he won a scholarship to the Royal College of Music to train as an opera singer. He pursued this career for some ten years, performing with major companies such as Sadlers Wells, D'Oyley Carte and the English National Opera. However, he grew tired of 'living out of a suitcase' and retrained as a probation officer, a job which he continued doing until he retired.

Frank Wilson

Gunner in the Royal Navy

When the Germans invaded Russia (then known as the Soviet Union, or USSR) in June 1941, Churchill promised to give what aid we could to this unwilling, recalcitrant ally. Much as he detested communism, he realised that if the Germans were fighting the Russians they would be less interested in invading Britain, and this proved to be the case. It made sense, therefore, to help Russia as best we could.

However, this meant sending convoys through the Arctic Ocean to the ports of Archangel and Murmansk, a highly dangerous journey, for two reasons. Firstly, because it involved passing close to occupied Norway and German-friendly Finland, from which aircraft and U Boats could launch constant attacks, and secondly because of the ferocious Arctic Ocean, where it was not uncommon for waves to be sixty feet high and ships could be smashed to pieces.

In winter it was bitterly cold. 20 degrees of frost was normal, sometimes even 50 degrees. Everything on deck would be covered with a thick layer of ice, which had to be constantly chopped off or the weight could eventually over-topple the ship, and to touch anything metal, even inside the ship, was to risk instant leaving your skin behind. It was sometimes too cold to sleep when off watch. The men could not wash and kept their clothes on day and night, on journeys that could last up to six weeks. Anyone who ended up in the water would be dead within two minutes. It was not for nothing that Churchill called it "the worst journey in the world."

Frank Wilson from Chesterfield joined the navy as a boy seaman aged 15 in 1939. Having done his training at HMS Ganges and HMS Collingwood, he went to sea at the age of 17. In total he made eight journeys to Russia, and he managed to survive with only the loss of his back teeth as a result of a bullet through his cheek, for which he had to wait a fortnight for treatment. He served on HMS Activity, a merchant ship converted to be an escort aircraft carrier, manning the Oerlikon anti-aircraft gun.

The MAC (Merchant Aircraft Carrier) ships were able to provide air cover for the convoys, but the pilots required a high degree of skill to fly to and from them. The flight decks were perilously short and landing on a pitching deck was a dangerous business. The aircraft most commonly flown was the Swordfish, a biplane which looked as if it had been left over from the First World War but which was in fact an extremely tough machine which could carry rockets and torpedoes and had a distinguished record against enemy warships and U-boats. However, its open cockpit offered little protection against the bitter cold, and the crews could suffer hypothermia. If they got lost in fog or ran out of fuel and had to ditch in the sea, they stood no chance of survival.

When the convoys arrived in Murmansk, far from being welcomed as allies bringing desperately needed weapons and supplies, they were greeted with suspicion and hostility, and usually they did not go ashore. To be fair, the people were very frightened, as the Germans were only a few miles away, and the city was being bombed night and day from air bases in Finland. After the war the Soviet government did show its gratitude by awarding the convoy crews medals for their courageous support. Some five thousand men died on the Arctic convoys but their contribution to the Russian war effort was immense. A normal convoy had about thirty ships, each carrying around 10,000 tons of cargo. Even allowing for losses due to enemy action, this meant that a significant amount of much-needed materials got through. Without that aid, Russia might well have lost the war, and then Hitler

Frank Wilson RN

The Arctic convoys 1941-45

would have turned his attention on Britain and carried out the invasion that he had postponed in 1940. As Frank said, "I don't think a lot of people realise what would have happened if we had not been doing these convoys. If it had not been for them the outcome of the war could have been very different. We would be speaking German now."

Frank's war service was not entirely on the Arctic convoys. His first journeys were across the Atlantic escorting merchant fleets to Halifax, Nova Scotia and other ports in Canada and the USA. Later in the war he was sent to the very different climate of the Far East, where he served on HMS Berwick. Their job was to patrol the seas between Australia and Ceylon (now Sri Lanka) to refuel.

Frank served in the Navy until 1949. He had signed on as a 'seven plus five' man, i.e. seven years full service and five in the reserves. His time as a boy seaman did not count. After he left the Navy he joined the merchant service and continued at sea until 1955, when he had to leave after an accident in which he smashed both elbows. He had climbed up a mast to change a bulb in one of the riding lights and was blown off by the strong wind. He had twelve month in hospital in Baltimore and New York.

In 2012 the Russian Embassy wrote to survivors of the Arctic

There were 78 convoys between August 1941 and May 1945, involving about 1400 merchant ships that delivered vital supplies to the Soviet Union – 85 merchant vessels and 16 RN warships were sunk. German losses included one battleship, at least 30 U-Boats and a large number of aircraft.

Convoys to say it intended to award them yet another decoration, the Medal of Ushakov, as a symbol of the country's gratitude. This was a medal for bravery in naval warfare, named after a famous Russian admiral. Why Russia wanted to make this award nearly seventy years later, especially as it had already awarded medals after the war, is an interesting question, but the British Foreign Office blocked the plan on the grounds that medals for service to a foreign country could not be given unless the action was within the last five years. Following an article in the Derbyshire Times the case was taken up by Chesterfield MP Toby Perkins and others, and eventually the ruling was rescinded, although Frank has yet to receive the medal!

Walter Randle

Able Seaman in the Merchant Navy

Walter Randle, from Derby, was an adventurous youth. In 1939, at the age of twelve, he and two of his mates decided that it would be a bit of fun to run away from home. They clambered aboard the wagon of a goods train at Derby station, and for a couple of hours they travelled in this surprisingly uncomfortable mode of transport until they came to a halt. They had no idea where they were, but found out they were in Mansfield. Having brought neither food nor money, they stole some bread from a shop and milk from a passing float, then 'borrowed' some bikes and cycled back to Derby. Walter's machine developed a puncture, which made progress slow and difficult. When he got home he expected to be in trouble with his grandma, with whom he lived, but to his surprise she said not a word!

However, Walter's youthful escapades got him into conflict with the law, and eventually he found himself in front of the magistrates, who suggested that to avoid further trouble he should join a training ship and prepare for a life at sea. He agreed to this, and from 1941 to 1943 he went through a rigorous programme of training for the Merchant Navy. Discipline was strict; a boy caught smoking would have to eat the cigarette, if he swore he would have to stand for an hour with his mouth stuffed with carbolic soap, if he went AWOL (absent without leave) he would be flogged, and if he went AWOL and made a nuisance of himself he would have to 'run the gauntlet' between two lines of boys armed with sticks.

Walter not only survived this harsh regime, he finished the course as Top Boy. At the age of sixteen years and one month he went to sea as a cabin boy, the youngest person to subsequently qualify for the War Medal 1939-45. His ship was part of a convoy from Belfast to New York. This was the first of a remarkable series of voyages across almost every ocean of the world: the Atlantic convoys to North America, the Arctic convoys to Murmansk in Russia, the

Mediterranean convoys to Malta, Cyprus, Israel, Italy and North Africa, convoys to Sierra Leone and down the west coast of Africa to Cape Town, and to Brazil and Venezuela in South America. He even went on a five-week unescorted journey via the Panama Canal to Australia and New Zealand. Nowadays we are able to travel almost anywhere in the world, and think nothing of it; to a working-class lad from Derby in those days it must have been the adventure of a lifetime.

Walter believed he had been blessed with more than his fair share of good luck in life. Amazingly, in all the thousands of miles he travelled, none of his ships was sunk. This may have been because by 1943 the development of ASDIC, an echo-sounding device that enabled enemy submarines to be detected and attacked, had greatly reduced the amount of shipping that was lost to the U-boats. Nevertheless, Walter saw several ships torpedoed and witnessed the harrowing sight of survivors in lifeboats or struggling in oily water, knowing that no ship dared stop to pick them up or they would have been sitting targets for enemy submarines or aircraft.

Ironically, one of the most dangerous situations that Walter found himself in was not at sea but while on shore leave in Cape Town. Ever adventurous, he and a pal decided to go into District Six with a couple of coloured girls they had met in a bar. Although this was the pre-apartheid era, there was even then strict racial segregation in South Africa and District Six was definitely not an area for whites to venture into. They went with the girls into a house full of black men playing cards, and very quickly realised by the looks that were exchanged around the room that they were in danger. They made to leave, but the girls started to kick up a fuss. Suddenly, as the two lads made for the door, a huge man appeared, obviously intent on stopping them. Walter reached for the nearest solid object, which was a heavy metal ornament, and smashed it down on the man's head. This stunned him sufficiently for them to get out of the house, and they ran for their lives at a speed which would have undoubtedly won them an Olympic Gold Medal! They flagged down a passing bus and leapt aboard. Once again, Walter's luck had come to his rescue.

Walter remained in the Merchant Navy until July 1947, by which time, still only twenty, he had worked his way up from cabin boy to Able Seaman. He did an amazing variety of jobs, able to turn his hand successfully to almost anything. He worked on the railways, drove a lorry, ran a grocery business. He took up judo, gained a black belt and became an instructor. He took up ballroom dancing, became a champion and then a dancing teacher. He outlived two wives, married for a third time and had nine children, three of them out of wedlock!

A truly remarkable and highly colourful character, Walter is currently writing his life story, which should be a fascinating read!

Frank Stone

Prisoner of War in Stalagluft III

Frank Stone, from Hathersage, Derbyshire, probably holds the record for the shortest operational career in the history of the RAF. Just six weeks after joining, standing in for a sick rear gunner despite being completely untrained, he was shot down on his second bombing mission. He was captured and spent the next five years in a German prison camp.

Having joined the RAF on 14 May 1940, his eighteenth birthday, he spent four weeks 'square bashing' at Cardington before being selected for aircrew training as a navigator. This was to take place in Canada starting in September, so having a few weeks to fill in he was sent to 83 Squadron at RAF Scampton, later to be the base of the 'Dam Busters, and where the flight commander was Guy Gibson, who would lead the famous raid on the German dams in 1943. It was an operational station flying Hampden bombers. He was told to 'make himself useful and acclimatise to RAF life.'

He was invited to try some gunnery practice, and he must have made a good impression because a few days later, quite unexpectedly, he was asked if he would like to go on a mission! The Hampden carried two rear gunners, an upper and a lower, and the lower one was on sick leave. Despite his lack of training, Frank eagerly agreed to go in his place and squeezed himself into the cramped interior of the 'flying suitcase, as the narrow-bodied Hampden was nicknamed. It was a mine-laying operation in the Baltic, from which they returned unscathed. Frank was thrilled at having done a real mission so soon, but somewhat miffed not to be invited afterwards with the rest of the crew for bacon and eggs in the Sergeants' Mess. Being only a humble 'erk' (Aircraftman 2nd Class) he was not allowed in!

His chance for a second mission came a few nights later, this time a bombing raid on Ludwigshafen. Unfortunately, this time their luck ran out, and there would be no bacon and eggs for any of them. The starboard engine was hit by flak, which meant that the electronics were disabled and they could not release their bombs. Flying on one engine, the pilot tried to reach unoccupied France, but they continued to lose height, and eventually, over the Black Forest, he gave the order to bale out. Frank opened the escape hatch and was about to jump when he was seized from behind by the other rear gunner and pulled back. They were too low, and had he jumped his parachute would not have had time to open. He owed his life to his fellow gunner.

They crash landed in the dense forest. Miraculously the unreleased bombs did not go off and they escaped unhurt from the aircraft, apart from the navigator who had been thrown out of the front and broken his leg. They had not gone far before they were picked up by a couple of farmers who were armed and searching for them. They were handed over to the Luftwaffe, the German Air Force, who looked after all captured RAF airmen.

Frank was sent to Stalagluft I, a cold, windswept camp on the Baltic which housed 500 officers and 1500 other ranks. At first he worked in the cookhouse, and later was ordered to go into the nearby town to join a working party laying gas mains, and here he encountered unexpected kindness from the local people. One lady outside whose house he was working gave him coffee and cakes, another put food in the pocket of his jacket that was hanging on her door. Perhaps they had sons who were away fighting for their country, and took pity on this young boy who was a prisoner in a foreign land a long way from home.

When this job was finished, Frank worked briefly in a gasworks, which he found very unpleasant, so he applied to be an orderly in the officers' compound. The officers received eleven marks a week from which they could buy tobacco, razor blades and other necessities, and Frank's job was to make purchases for them, collect rations and keep their accommodation clean and tidy.

It was every prisoner's duty to escape. Though only a tiny number actually made a 'home run' to England, the many who did break out kept thousands of German soldiers busy searching for them and therefore diverted from the front line. Despite the fact that recaptured escapees had to spend two weeks in the 'cooler' on bread and water, there were many attempts from this camp. These was made difficult

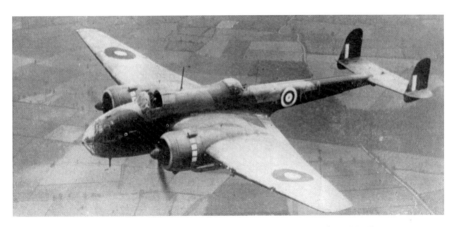

A Handley Page Hampden bomber, pictured in 1942

by the sandy soil and the high water table, which meant that tunnels could be no more than four feet deep. In all 48 tunnels were dug, and at one time there were so many recaptured escapees that there was a waiting list for the cooler!

Some had managed to get aboard ships going to neutral Sweden, so it was decided that the camp needed to be moved somewhere a long way from the sea. In March 1943 they were transferred to Stalagluft III, in eastern Germany, between Berlin and the Czech border. However even before the move, escape plans were being made, and Frank volunteered to be in the advance party preparing the site, so that he could find out where the seismographic microphones were located. These were hidden in the ground to detect the sound of tunnelling. To avoid detection, it was decided that the tunnels would have to be thirty feet deep.

It was Squadron Leader Roger Bushell, known as Big X, who conceived the idea of digging three tunnels simultaneously, so that if one was discovered the Germans would not expect any others to be in progress. All efforts were concentrated exclusively on these three, which were named Tom, Dick and Harry, so that the word 'tunnel' would never be heard by the 'ferrets', German guards whose job was to eavesdrop on conversations in the hope of picking up clues about escape attempts.

The digging was done by volunteers who worked in the most appalling conditions. The tunnels were hot and airless, and the soil was so sandy that the diggers were in constant risk of being buried alive. The only light was provided by lamps made by skimming the fat off soup and pouring it into fish paste tins where it solidified. The smell from these made the air in the tunnels even more foul.

Ingenious solutions for these problems were found. A pump was made from kit bags to bring fresh air into the tunnels. To shore them up, bed boards were used, which each man had to donate from his bed, leaving just enough to support his mattress. Some local workmen were careless enough to leave a length of electric cable lying around, and this was rapidly spirited away and used to provide light in the tunnel, which eliminated the smell as well as giving a much brighter light. Getting rid of the excavated soil was the job of the 'penguins', who would carry the soil in bags under their trousers. They would nonchalantly stroll round the camp with their hands in their pockets, gradually releasing the soil from the bags as they did so.

Frank lived in the hut from which 'Harry' started, and his job was to sweep away all traces of soil off the floor so that the 'ferrets' would not be suspicious. He also 'entertained' Glemnitz, the chief 'ferret' to coffee in his room to keep him diverted. Nevertheless, despite the best efforts of the 'stooges' who kept a constant lookout, 'Tom' was discovered and blown up, the force of the explosion almost lifting the roof off the hut! 'Dick' had to be aborted when it was learned that the camp was to be extended into the area where it was planned to emerge, leaving 'Harry' as the sole remaining tunnel. Bushell's idea of building three tunnels had paid off.

March 24, 1944 was chosen as the escape night. Of the 800 men who had contributed to the escape, 200 were selected. The tunnel diggers and fluent German speakers had priority, the rest drew lots. Frank was on the reserve list but was not selected.

Unfortunately, it did not go according to plan. The first problem was that the wooden trap door at the far end had swollen and took over an hour to force open. Then, as the men began to emerge, it became obvious that they were not in the forest as planned but ten feet away in open country. This was not due to a miscalculation; it was just that, unknown to them, the tree line curved in the centre, leaving the tunnel exit fully exposed. Under the bright arc lights, and with sentries patrolling the perimeter, each man had to wait until both guards had their backs to him before scrambling out and dashing into the forest. This greatly slowed things down. Then came an air raid, which caused all the lights to be extinguished for some time, and by dawn only 76 men had got out. The escape ended when one of the sentries started to walk towards the trees, possibly to relieve himself, and almost fell over the man just climbing out. The alarm was raised and the escape aborted.

Three men, two Norwegians and a Dutchman, all fluent in German, made it back to England. Fifteen were returned to camp and five were sent to Sachsenhausen Concentration Camp, possibly to be ransomed. Amazingly, they dug a tunnel and escaped, but were recaptured. They all survived.

There was a terrible sequel to the escape. Hitler, infuriated when he learned of the escape, ordered fifty of the recaptured men to be shot as a deterrent to others. The news was received with horror back at the camp, and even the guards were ashamed. Such an action went totally against the Geneva Convention, which the Luftwaffe had scrupulously observed in its treatment of prisoners. The commandant even paid out of his own pocket for a memorial to the murdered men. Although all privileges had been withdrawn in the aftermath of the escape, they were immediately reinstated when the news of the executions came.

On 18 January 1945, as the Red Army closed in on Germany, the PoWs were given one hour's notice and marched out of the camp. It was one of the coldest nights on record. In this bitter cold, with two feet if snow on the ground, they marched for the next five days. They were then taken in cattle trucks to a camp near Bremen, where they stayed until April, when they were marched on to Lubeck, but refused to enter the town as they heard there had been an outbreak of typhus. They had neither food nor shelter, and survived by bartering what they had with the local people. They were billeted on the farm of an estate similar to Chatsworth.

Then, on 3 May, the British Army arrived. They were now free, and were told to take over the farm from the guards. However, it felt an anti-climax, as there was no transport to take them away. They had nothing with which to celebrate VE Day; it was just another day for them. Finally, the transport arrived and on 11 May Frank was flown home in a Lancaster, four years and nine months after becoming a prisoner of war.

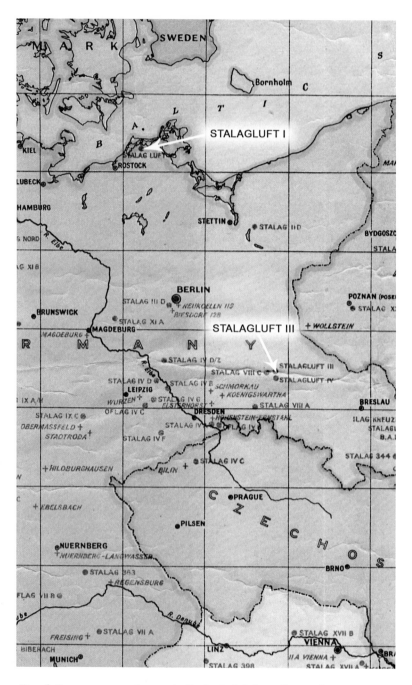

Frank Stone was a prisoner in Stalagluft I from September 1940 until he was transferred to Stalagluft III in March 1943. He was freed by the advancing British Army on 3 May 1945.

During his time in captivity he had studied navigation in the hope of fulfilling his ambition to train for aircrew, but the RAF was now winding down and the only trade on offer was lorry driver! He declined, left the RAF and went into the Civil Service.

Frank had not considered his wartime life to have been of much interest to anyone, but many years later his daughter asked him to give a talk about his time as a PoW at her Young Farmers' Club, the guest speaker having let them down. This was received with great interest, and soon other groups were asking Frank to give his talk to them. He still continues to do so, even at the age of 90! He has appeared on the BBC's 'The One Show', with Kate Humble on 'Who Do You Think You Are?' and he has made a DVD of his talk, proceeds from the sale of which go to the Bomber Command Memorial Fund.

Frank has also revisited the site of the camp, much of which has now reverted to forest. One hut has been rebuilt and now stands as a museum and education centre. The entrance to 'Harry' is marked with a stone slab, and for each of the 76 escapees there is a slab bearing his name.

The escape from Stalag Luft III has become one of the legends of the Second World War. It was immortalised in the 1963 film 'The Great Escape', which, when completed, was shown to an invited audience of ex Pows, who expressed satisfaction that it was generally an accurate portrayal of the escape. However, being a Hollywood movie it had to show the Americans playing a far greater role than they actually did, and possibly the most ludicrous scene was where Steve McQueen, dressed not in uniform but in clothes that would not come into fashion for another twenty years (Chinos and a sweatshirt!) vaults on a motorbike over the barbed wire border fence.

Being a prisoner-or-war was an immensely frustrating experience. Though not badly treated, they had to live in Spartan accommodation on meagre rations, their world circumscribed by a double wall of barbed wire, ever conscious that the war was being fought without them. It was not surprising that they devoted so much time and energy to escaping, not only because it was their duty to escape but also because it relieved the mind-numbing boredom of camp life. Being aircrew, they were all men of reasonable intelligence, and many had high levels of skill which they put to good use. With incredible ingenuity, they worked out ways to overcome the tunnelling problems they encountered, as well as making civilian clothes, maps, compasses (which Frank helped to make) and forged documents.

Much to his regret, Frank did not have the chance to escape, though he helped others to do so. However, when he learned of the fate of fifty of the escapees his disappointment must have turned to relief. He at least returned home alive and unhurt (and, amazingly, five inches taller!). Had he not been shot down but gone on to become a navigator on bombing raids, his chances of surviving the war would have been slim. Bomber Command had the highest casualty rate of any branch of the armed forces. Of the 125,000 men who volunteered for aircrew, no less than 55,500 were killed, a fatality rate of 44%. Only 17% of bomber crews completed a full tour of thirty missions.

The fact that Frank spent five years in a prison camp does not mean he did not play his part in the war effort. Escaping meant that the enemy had to tie down thousands of troops who would otherwise be on the front line, and though he himself was not able to escape, he helped others to do so. Escaping was the only way they could fight back, and it was highly effective.

Frank has no regrets about his time in captivity. Far from being wasted years, they were an opportunity to mix with men from a variety of backgrounds and nations, and to experience the camaraderie of those going through a shared ordeal. In a way, these were Frank's years in the University of Life.

When it was over, he came home, got married, had a family and is still alive and well at 90. Had he not been shot down in August 1940 his name might well be one of the 55,000 inscribed on the newly-opened Bomber Command Memorial in London, a memorial that he helped to create.

Cover of a DVD produced by Frank Stone, which tells the story of his 'Great Escape'.

Norman Crookes MBE, DFC

Navigator/Radar Operator in the RAF

The Distinguished Flying Cross (DFC) was awarded for "acts of valour, courage or devotion to duty whilst flying on active service against the enemy". Over 20,000 were awarded during the Second World War, more than any other medal for bravery, which reflects the enormous dangers faced by those who flew in combat, and the courage they showed in doing so. Some 1500 were awarded a second DFC, while an exceptional few, 45 in number, were awarded a third. One of these was a Chesterfield man, Squadron Leader Norman Crookes, who, in addition to this incredible achievement, was also awarded the American DFC!

The son of a builder, Norman was born in New Tupton, near Chesterfield, in 1920. This was the village on which a stick of bombs was jettisoned by a German bomber escaping pursuit. One of these bombs dropped on the roof of Norman's grandfather's shop, causing it to cave in. He was asleep in bed at the time, but miraculously escaped unharmed!

Norman was a a bright lad. He attended Tupton Hall Grammar School, where he was captain of the First X1 football team and Head Boy in 1938-39. He won a scholarship to Kings College, University of London, where he studied for an honours degree in history.

On 11 July 1941, at the end of his second year, he volunteered for the RAF, and was accepted for aircrew training. After navigation and radar training he joined 125 Squadron at Colerne, near Bath, as a radar operator/navigator on night fighters. He crewed up with pilot George 'Jamie' Jameson, a New Zealander, flying Beaufighters. At this stage he was a sergeant, but in October 1942 he was commissioned.

They had their first combat on 27 July 1942 when they shot down a Heinkel 111 near the oil refinery at Milford Haven. A week later they shot down a second Heinkel in the same area. Though flying at

Norman Crookes and his pilot Flt Lt 'Jamie' Jameson

night, the radar enabled Norman to 'see' the enemy aircraft and direct the pilot to it.

They were then sent to the Shetlands to try to combat the German weather reconnaissance aircraft flying out from Norway. On one occasion they suffered engine failure 150 miles out over the North Sea. They had a tense hour limping back on one engine, losing height all the time, fearing that they would end up in the cold sea, in which they would be unlikely to survive for more than a few minutes. They were down to 2000 feet when they reached land, and came down safely, much to their relief, and to the relief of Norman's mother, who had received a telegram informing her that Norman had been reported missing! Possibly Jamie's mother would have received one too, which would have been devastating news as two of her other sons had already been killed in action.

In February 1943, during the blitz on Swansea, they achieved their final success in a Beaufighter when they shot down a Dornier 217 over the Gower Peninsula. Norman and Jamie were then sent for a spell to train night fighter crews. In January 1944 they were transferred to 488, a New Zealand squadron, and converted to flying Mosquitos. They had to wait until 24 June for their first success, when they shot down a Messerschmitt 410 over Bayeux. The D-Day invasion had taken place by now, and their role was to patrol the beach head area. Four nights later they brought down a Junkers 88 over Caen. The two men had now achieved 'ace' status (five enemy shot down) and had each been awarded the DFC.

However, their greatest achievement was yet to come. In the early hours of 30 July 1944, flying over Saint-Lo, they shot down no less than four enemy aircraft in half an hour, an achievement unequalled by any Allied fighter crew in North West Europe. The first victim was a Junkers 88, which a short burst of cannon fire sent plummeting to the ground. Almost immediately, Norman picked up a second contact, another Ju88. Despite its desperate manoeuvres it fell victim to a burst of cannon fire and crashed. Resuming their patrol, they spotted yet another Ju88 flying in and out of cloud. Norman tracked it on his radar and they closed in and shot it down. Then he picked up two more contacts and directed Jamie to the nearest, a Dornier 217. That too was shot down.

Their action was hailed throughout the RAF as the finest night fighter sortie of the war. Jamie was immediately awarded the DSO and Norman a bar to his DFC. However, their satisfaction was tempered by the tragic news that Jamie's father had died. As stated earlier, his two brothers had recently been killed, and Jamie was sent back to New Zealand to help his mother run the family farm.

Before he departed they shot down two more Ju88s. In all they had destroyed eleven enemy aircraft. The squadron then moved to France and Norman teamed up with another New Zealander, Flying Officer Ray Jeffs. On their first night patrol together they shot down a Dornier 217 over Caen. They then saw service in the American sector during the Battle of the Bulge, where the Germans were pushing the Americans back. Just before Christmas they attacked and damaged a Ju88 but did not know if they had shot it down. It was not until the 1990s that a researcher confirmed that it had been destroyed! For his service in support of the US forces Norman was awarded the American DFC.

On April 24, 1945 Norman flew his final patrol, which was over Berlin, and the squadron was disbanded almost as soon as the war ended. On leaving, Norman was awarded a second bar to his DFC for "his unfailing devotion to duty". He spent his last year of service as a Squadron Leader in command of a Ground Control Unit whose purpose was to guide an aircraft down to a safe landing in poor visibility.

Norman would like to have stayed on in the RAF but, ironically, his request was denied because he was discovered to be colour blind! He could have had a ground job, but he only wanted to fly. He was demobbed in October 1946, and returned to university to complete his degree and gain his Teaching Diploma. This involved considerable hardship, as he was now married and living in London was not cheap. After qualifying he took a post as history master at Brockley Grammar School in Lewisham, and a few years later returned to Derbyshire as Head of Clay Cross Boys' School from 1957 to 1961 and of William Rhodes Boys' School, Chesterfield from 1961 to 1981, when he retired.

He took a keen interest in the Air Training Corps. He was CO of 768 Squadron at Brockley, of 2326 Squadron in Clay Cross and of the squadron he formed at William Rhodes. He was Training Officer for the Derbyshire Wing, and later, as a civilian, he was chairman of the East Midlands Wing. He was appointed MBE for services to the ATC in 1974.

Norman's first wife, Kathleen, whom he married in 1944, died in 1987. His second wife, Sheila, describes their time together as "twenty three very happy years." He died on 17 April 2012, aged 91.

Norman Crookes was a man who succeeded in life by applying himself wholeheartedly to whatever he did. From a working class background he gained a place at grammar school and went on to be Head Boy and football captain, won a scholarship to university, had a highly distinguished war record, became a headmaster of two schools and was honoured for his dedication to the ATC.

Sheila once asked him how he felt about his war service. Like most airmen he had lost friends, one in particular who he was close to, but his attitude was that there was a job to be done and you just got on with it. Naturally you would keenly feel the loss of friends, but it did not stop you doing what had to be done.

In view of Norman's outstanding war record, it is perhaps surprising that he is not more well known. The answer is that he was a modest man, who did not seek publicity. His achievements were well known in RAF circles, and when he was in uniform his DFC and two bars spoke for themselves. But he did not seek fame or glory. He had done his job well, and that was enough.

His ability to do a job well was also shown in his work as a teacher. Many of his former pupils contacted Sheila after his death to say how much they had enjoyed being taught by him. One in particular, a former pupil of Brockley Grammar School, commented on his kind, supportive approach, which contrasted with the sarcasm and humiliation that most of the other masters employed. The fact that he became a headmaster after only nine years is an indication of his outstanding ability.

I knew of Norman Crookes through a mutual friend, but I never met him. Sadly, he died just as I was starting this project, and I am indebted to his wife, Sheila, for providing me with invaluable information about the life of this remarkable man.

Elsa Fierman

Leading Aircraftwoman, WAAF

Elsa Fierman, nee Greaves, was 18 when she was called up into the Women's Auxiliary Air Force (WAAF) in 1942. She was the fifth of nine children brought up in a two-up-two-down terraced house in Sheffield, and it was not until she went into the Air Force that she had a bed to herself. Up till then she had slept sandwiched between two of her sisters!

Before being called up Elsa worked in Woolworths in the centre of Sheffield, and recalls travelling to work through streets of bomb-damaged buildings, overturned trams and sometimes dead bodies laid out on the pavement.

Unlike today's well-travelled youngsters, Elsa had never been further from home than Skegness. When she was told to report to somewhere in Wiltshire she barely knew where it was. On her first night in barracks she felt a very long way from the warmth of her large family, though she says she did not join in the general weeping that she could hear all around her.

After basic training she spent ten weeks in Skegness awaiting the call to start her training as an MT (Motor Transport) driver. During these weeks there was little to do but enjoy the warmth of that beautiful summer. Unfortunately the beach, like all beaches around Britain, was barricaded with barbed wire as a defence against invasion, and was therefore inaccessible.

From there Elsa went to Morecambe for her driver training. Up till then, not only had she never driven a car, she had never even sat inside one! This was long before the advent of such aids as power steering, and driving was physically demanding work, especially when she graduated to three-ton lorries. There were no synchromesh gearboxes in those days, and she had to learn the difficult art of 'double de-clutching' when changing down. Getting it wrong could result in a ruined gearbox. Changing a tyre, both on cars and lorries, was another of the skills she had to learn. She took her driving test on a busy Saturday lunchtime in Morecambe, an extremely nerve-racking experience.

Her training completed, Elsa was posted to RAF Rufforth, near York, where she would spend the next two and a half years. This was the home of 1663 Heavy Conversion Unit (HCU), where aircrew in the final stage of their training learned to handle four-engined heavy bombers such as the Halifax. One of Elsa's duties including ferrying crews to and from the aircraft, which were usually dispersed over a wide area in case the airfield was bombed. Delivery driving was another of her jobs, and as all the signposts and name boards of every town and village had been removed at the beginning of the war, this was quite a challenge, and involved familiarising oneself with maps and routes before starting on a journey.

A particularly unpleasant memory for Elsa was the Grasslands Farm crash. It was to be expected that at an airfield where fledgling crews were learning to handle very large aircraft there would be accidents, but this one was particularly horrific as it involved the deaths not only of all but one of the crew but also of three civilians. On the late evening of 16 November 1944, the fog started

Elsa Fierman, left, and a friend, drivers at RAF Rufforth, York. Elsa's discharge papers described her as 'Of outstanding capability in respect of driving ...'

unexpectedly to rise. A Halifax piloted by Flight Lieutenant W J Matthews was coming in to land, but he was confused by the fog and came in to the left of the runway and struck the roof of Grasslands Farm, killing the farmer, Mr George Hildreth, his wife Mary and his son Kenneth. The farmhouse and outbuildings burst into flames and most of the cattle and sheep were sprayed with burning petrol. The crash crew rushed to the scene, and were joined by the local fire brigade. Between them they managed to limit the damage to the property. Elsa was told to stand by in case anyone needed to be ferried around. Her abiding memory is the smell of burned animals.

During her time at Rufforth Elsa met a man with whom she fell in love. Unfortunately he was married, and the relationship came to an end when the war ended. He was, says Elsa, the only man she ever really loved. She was obviously a popular girl, as she received three other proposals before finally deciding to get married.

Elsa was demobbed at the end of 1945 with the rank of Leading Aircraftwoman and her discharge document contained a commendation which read, "Of outstanding capability in respect of driving, keen on maintenance, careful and constantly cheerful in all her undertakings." She was asked to stay on with the rank of Corporal, but decided to return to civilian life. The shy young girl who had joined up in 1942 was now a confident extrovert, and the experience has stood her in good stead for the rest of her life. Though not in a combat role, her wartime life had not been without its dangers, as Rufforth airfield was bombed from time to time. Only a few miles from York, it was a prime target for enemy aircraft jettisoning their bombs to escape pursuit by night fighters.

Elsa found it very difficult to adjust to civilian life after the war, and for some time afterwards would have screaming fits in the night, prompted by her memories of the fire. She returned to work at Woolworths, where she became head girl, and later for Wigfalls, a Sheffield department store, employing her driving skills delivering radios, and later televisions. She married in 1947 and had two children. She is now a widow, has four grandchildren and three great grandchildren, and lives in Chesterfield.

THE HOME FRONT

No previous war in British history had relied so heavily on the contribution of the civilian population to achieve victory. In the 1914-18 war a large number of women had worked in factories and on farms to replace the men at the front, and such was their contribution to the final victory that Prime Minister Herbert Asquith was moved to praise their efforts and support their right to vote, whereas before the war he had been adamantly opposed to it. But in the Second World War not only did thousands of women go into the workplace to do the jobs traditionally done by men, but men too old or unfit for military service, or in reserved occupations, were also required to do war work, or serve as air raid wardens, first aid workers, firewatchers or in the Home Guard. Some were drafted into the coal mines. Others were engaged in highly secret code-breaking work which enabled military commanders to know what the enemy was planning .Everybody 'did their bit'.

Never before had the civilians suffered so many casualties. There had been bombing raids on London from 1915 onwards, but on a far smaller scale than in the next war. Not only was London relentlessly attacked in 1940-41, but so also were Coventry, Birmingham, Sheffield, and most other industrial towns and cities. The V1 and V2 attacks in 1944-45 only added to the suffering of the war-weary population.

It was feared that aerial bombardment would break the morale of the civilian population, but in fact it had the opposite effect, making people all the more determined not to give in. Even the continuous nightly bombing during the 'Blitz' failed to crack public morale. In our area, Derby, in spite of having the Rolls Royce factory manufacturing aero engines, got off relatively lightly, but Sheffield, with its vast steel works, was heavily bombed.

I interviewed eight women and two men who were engaged in war work as civilians. Some worked in factories, others on the land,

and one ran a NAAFI canteen. One of the men was a 'Bevin Boy', conscripted into the coal mines rather than the forces. While the civilians did not face the same dangers as the men in the armed services, the war could not have been won without the vital backup that they provided.

Bessie Summerfield

Armaments Factory Worker

When Bessie's call up came in 1942 she had to choose between the armed forces and war production work. Her mother did not want her to go away from home so she opted for factory work, although that took her to Leicester, too far to commute from her home in Chesterfield. She trained as a grinder, which involved taking metal cylinders and grinding them down to the required size, a very precise task for which she learned to use a micrometer.

She then went even further away from home, to Northampton. Here she made undercarriage parts for Lancaster bombers. The cylinders were often coated with a thick layer of rust, but at the end of the process they were mirror-bright. It was hard work doing twelve-hour shifts, six days a week, but she enjoyed it. It was essential work, a vital contribution to the war effort.

While she was in Northampton, she and a friend were walking through the town one evening when they heard what sounded like an extremely loud motorcycle. However, the noise was coming from the sky and people were running in all directions in complete panic. Suddenly the noise stopped. Several seconds went by, and then there was a thunderous explosion.

It was a V1 Flying Bomb, one of thousands that were launched against Britain from June 1944 onwards, Hitler's desperate attempt to turn the tide of the war in his favour by launching these indiscriminate terror weapons on a war-weary civilian population. The vast majority were aimed at London, but some were directed at more distant targets. This one was probably intended for the munitions factory in Northampton. Fortunately it landed in a farmer's field and the only fatality was one of his cows!

Shortly after this she and a colleague were late returning to work after lunch and received a reprimand from their boss. However, they had been prevented from crossing the road by an endless military convoy of lorries full of men who looked exhausted, and in some cases wounded. These were the casualties of the recent D Day landings on the beaches of Normandy, and it was a grim reminder of the fierce fighting that was taking place on the other side of the Channel as our armies began the long hard struggle recapture occupied Europe from the Germans.

Later that year Bessie returned to her home town to work at Chesterfield Cylinders, known locally as 'The Tube Works', where she made shell cases. When the war came to an end she returned to Robinsons. In January 1946 her fiancée Jack returned after four years with the RAF in Burma, and three months later they married.

Bessie enjoyed the work. Having been employed at Robinsons in Chesterfield before being called up, she was used to the factory environment. It was a very male world, but the women were treated with respect, and the occasional bottom-pinching was laughed off as harmless fun. It would never have occurred to them to claim sexual harassment!

Something she now recalls with amusement was opening her wage packet one week and being amazed to find a white £5 note. Neither she nor her family had ever seen one before!

Nora Caldwell

Textile Factory Worker

Orphaned at the age of six, Nora was living with her aunt and uncle in the South Yorkshire village of Barugh Green, near Barnsley when the war broke out. She was nine years old and still at school, and she remembers no longer being able to eat oranges or bananas. Our merchant ships were under attack from U-boats, and every inch of storage space was required for essential war materials. Sweets were rationed, so instead she took a carrot to school to chew on during playtime, something that would cause today's children would turn their noses up! She also recalls the Anderson shelter in the garden. Unfortunately they were on clay soil, and because her uncle had dug their so deep it was constantly flooded, so they had to go and share their neighbour's shelter.

Nora recalls being in the shelters under the school playground, all the children huddled together listening to the terrifying sound of bombs whistling down and exploding. Although there was not a great deal of bombing in her immediate area, the chemical works at nearby Darton were a target, and Sheffield, a few miles away, with its vast steelworks, was frequently bombed.

She also had to get used to the blackout, but so far from being scared she and her friends revelled in the chance to get up to mischief in the dark! Far more frightening were the thick fogs that were common in those days. On one occasion her uncle failed to return from work at tea time. They set out in search of him, but some hours had gone by before he was found in the middle of a field, having got off the bus and completely lost his way!

Nora's contribution to the war effort began as soon as she left school at fourteen, when she went to work at Hinchliffe's Mills in Denby Dale, a half hour's bus ride away. This was a spinning factory making clothing for the forces, and Nora's job was to operate the machines which teased out the raw wool. It was difficult work, but she was very versatile, and was soon able to do almost every job in the factory, including those previously done by men. She eventually became a fitter's mate, a position for which she had to be carefully chosen to suit the man she would be working with. She was soon able to strip down the heavy machines, clean them and put them back together.

What was it like for a young girl in this very male environment? "I enjoyed every minute!" said Nora. She was well regarded by the men, and the phrase "Nora will do it" became a common saying in the factory. Paid on piece work, she earned good wages, sometimes even more than her uncle, but as was the norm in those days she handed over her wage packet and was given half a crown (twelve and a half pence in decimal money) to spend.

Entertainments were much simpler in those days: whist drives, beetle drives, dances and the cinema were the standard fare, while radio kept people entertained at home as well as being the main source of war news. There were few military establishments in the area, and only the presence of soldiers on Rest and Recuperation (R and R) reminded them that most of the male population were in uniform. This was a mining area, and miners were classed as being in a reserved occupation. In fact there was nearby a hostel for 'Bevin Boys', young men who were conscripted into the mines rather than the armed forces to make up the shortfall in the workforce. The scheme was named after its founder, Minister of Labour Ernest Bevin.

With the end of the war, the men returned to the factory, but Nora worked on there until she got married in 1949. She now lives in Littleover, near Derby.

Joan Spicer

Aircraft Factory Worker

Joan's early life did little to prepare her for the factory work she would do during the war. She was born in a farm cottage where water was drawn from a well in a bucket and the toilet was at the bottom of a field. In 1937, when she was thirteen, the family moved to Birmingham, where her father, a trumpeter in a dance band, was offered work. She attended Birmingham Art College, where she was directed into window dressing at Isabel's, a very expensive fashion shop specialising in mink coats and fox fur stoles.

The first bombs that fell on Birmingham practically demolished the whole arcade. Arriving at work the next morning, she had to try to salvage what was left of the stock. They moved to a much smaller shop and most of the staff left. Because of electricity restrictions they were only allowed to open from 10 am to 4 pm.

Joan then received a letter stating that as she was only working 20 hours a week her services would be useful at a First Aid Post at the local swimming baths. It was here that she saw her first casualties when an incendiary bomb landed nearby. Several men rushed out with shovels and buckets to fight the flames, and some came back with terrible burns. It became a very busy post, and after the war she saw a letter in the local paper which said that the matron had received an award from the Queen for her services.

Joan's family, like many others, had an Anderson shelter in the garden. It faced their neighbour's, and one night an incendiary landed between the two shelters. The firemen shovelled earth off the roofs to smother the flames. After that they decided it was marginally safer to shelter indoors under the table.

A week after her eighteenth birthday, Joan was called up for war service and was told to report to the Vickers Armstrongs factory at Castle Bromwich, where Spitfires were built. Joan was one of eight girls who all started together. They were taught by a rather shy young

Joan Spicer (centre) with friends from the Vickers Armstrong Spitfire factory, Castle Bromwich

man to drill holes and put rivets in trays that held the radio sets that went into the aircraft, and in return they taught him dance steps!

It was a long day for Joan. She had to leave the house at 5.45 to be at work for 7 o'clock, and at the end of the day she was never home before 8 pm. Saturday was a half day, but sometimes she had to work four hours on a Sunday. Discipline was strict; if they clocked in two minutes late they were stopped fifteen minutes pay! They earned good money, but a third was deducted for tax, and as everything was on ration or coupons there was no pleasure in shopping.

Despite the long hours and the repetitive nature of the work, Joan enjoyed her time there, though when she was called up she had been horrified at the idea of working in a factory. The eight girls formed a tight-knit little group, and they would go to the cinema together at weekends or dancing, although most of the men they met were middle aged or foreign troops, especially Americans. They also went on holiday together in Llandudno.

Joan's sister Hilda was also called up for war work, but unlike

The reunion of the 'Spitfire Girls' in about 1996 ...

... and the report in the Birmingham Post.

Girls behind the Few: Castle Bromwich Spitfire workers Mary McKeever (left), Maureen Carr, Ruby Francis, Audrey Godrige, Doris Davis, Joan Spicer and Olive Johnson at only their second reunion in 50 years.　Picture/JOHN REAVENALL

Spitfire production girls meet up again

By STEPHEN HARRISON
The Birmingham Post

More than 50 years on, the memories came flooding back for the unsung heroines who helped to put thousands of Spitfires into the skies from a Birmingham factory.

Seven of the "girls" who worked on the production line at the old Vickers Armstrong factory, in Castle Bromwich, joined up for only their second reunion since the 1940s.

Now in their 70s, they first met up, in 1942.

Mrs Maureen Carr, who worked on the Spitfire's tailplane, said: "They were hard times, but they were good.

"They were long hours because we worked from seven in the morning till six in the even-

ing, and we did a five-and-a-half-day week apart from when we were pushed and did extra time. But we thoroughly enjoyed ourselves because we were good friends."

And Mrs Mary McKeever — who helped fit the plane's radio gear — said: "Mostly I was drilling holes, which was very boring. We just kept going — and still went out nearly every night to enjoy ourselves.

Yesterday's second gathering — at the Copt Heath Golf Club, near Solihull — was organised by Mrs Ruby Francis's husband Geoff.

He said: "They went their separate ways after the war, but always kept in touch with cards at Christmas.

"We had a reunion after 25 years, and I wanted to get them all together in one place again."

You must remember this: Audrey (left), Maureen, Joan and Doris take a stroll during a wartime break in Llandudno.

85

Joan she hated the job, which was in a foundry making moulds for components. However, her father sorted matters out for her by going to see the factory manager. He had just come from a rehearsal, and was in evening dress, which caused a few raised eyebrows as he walked through the offices. The manager was even more impressed when he was offered complimentary tickets for the next show. After that her sister worked in the offices!

It was while on holiday that Joan met Ernest, the man who would become her husband. He was serving in the RAF as a wireless operator on Stirling bombers, and at the time was based in Anglesey. They married after the war and had one son, Keith. Ernest continued to work in Birmingham until he was made redundant, and then he got a job in Sheffield. They bought a bungalow in Old Tupton, near Chesterfield, where Joan still lives.

The eight girls who worked together in the war stayed friends for the rest of their lives. They all married and, coincidentally, all had just one child!

Edna Gould

Overhead Crane Driver

Edna was one of nine children and grew up in the mining town of Clay Cross, near Chesterfield. During the early years of the war, she worked in a camp for evacuees from Derby in the nearby village of Ogston.

Then, in 1943, she went into the very male world of heavy industry when she got a job at Chesterfield Cylinders, known locally as the 'Tube Works'. At first she tested, by filling them with water, cylinders that would contain oxygen for airmen, but later she trained as an overhead crane driver. This was a very responsible job, as any mistakes on her part could have disastrous consequences. On one occasion, while stacking steel bars under instruction from a man on the ground, she felt he was not doing it correctly, but nevertheless carried out his instructions, and sure enough the stack fell. She came down out of the crane and gave him an 'earful', making it clear that she was not taking responsibility for his mistake!

It was a hot, dusty environment, and very noisy. In fact the only way to communicate was through sign language. For safety she had her hair in a snood (a hair net) and wore clogs on her feet because of the steel on the floor. On one occasion she went home in her work overalls, to the disgust of her father, who considered trousers unsuitable for a woman, until she pointed out that climbing up into a crane wearing a skirt was even more unsuitable! She had to work shifts, mornings (6 till 2), afternoons (2 till 10) and nights (10 till 6), seven days a week with no holidays. Many women worked there during the war, and as was normal, they were paid at a lower rate than the men for the same job, but when they complained to the union rep, they just got a mouthful of abuse!

Sometimes when the buses were not running due to the fog she had to walk the four miles home to Clay Cross. In case of attack she carried her 'secret weapon', a six-inch steel needle with a wooden handle, though fortunately she never needed to use it.

Like many other people at the time her family supplemented their food rations by growing vegetables and by keeping hens. When they had a glut of eggs they would preserve them in isinglass until they wanted them. They would also get a share of a pig when it was slaughtered, in exchange for food scraps which they donated.

Though no bombs dropped on Clay Cross, a German aircraft escaping pursuit jettisoned its deadly load on nearby Tupton, causing some twelve deaths and many injuries. Edna's father, an air raid warden, was involved in the rescue work

One night Edna accompanied one of her colleagues on a blind date and met the man who would become her husband. His name was Keith Gould, and he worked in one of the nearby collieries as a 'Bevin Boy' They married in April 1946. His story is told elsewhere.

Connie Davis

Clothing Factory Worker

At 99, Connie was the oldest of my interviewees. Her daughter, Marion, was kind enough to take me to the care home in Belper where she lives. It was not an easy interview as Connie is very deaf, and Marion had to act as 'interpreter' for me. At times it seemed as if the effort of recalling events of 70 years ago was almost too much. Nevertheless, an interesting story finally emerged.

Connie was born in Tottenham, North London, at the outbreak of the First World War. In 1932 she married, and she and her husband moved to Chingford, Essex. She worked at a clothing factory in Tottenham, and when war broke out the firm started making greatcoats and tunics for the army. Connie was a machinist and was designated a sample hand, which meant that she made the first garment which the others all copied. It was well-paid work; she received 45 shillings a week, whereas the standard rate for machinists was 24 shillings, but it was a long day, from 8 am to 6.45 pm. The workforce was entirely female.

She would always try to get home from work before the bombing raids started. In 1940-41 these were almost a nightly occurrence. One evening she was walking home and noticed it seemed to have gone very quiet. Not a soul was about. Suddenly she found herself being hustled into an air raid shelter. The bombers were about to arrive and she had been completely unaware of it! She also recalls the blackout, and frequently tripping on kerbs in the darkness.

Despite the risks, she would go into London every Saturday night to a dance hall in Stoke Newington, a journey that involved three bus rides, but she thought nothing of it. On one occasion she was touched on the arm and complimented on her dancing by none other than the famous band leader Victor Sylvester!

"...On one occasion she was touched on the arm and complimented on her dancing by none other than the famous band leader Victor Sylvester!"

In 1941 she and her husband decided to move to Ripley, in Derbyshire, partly to rejoin some neighbours who had moved up and partly to get away from the bombing. However, Derbyshire must have cast a spell on them, because instead of going back to London they stayed in Ripley for the rest of their lives.

Joan Stevens

Women's Land Army

Having survived the destruction of her home in a bombing raid, Joan decided in 1943 that she wanted to volunteer for the WAAF. However, she was still 17 and her father refused to give his consent, so she had to wait a further year until she was 18. But luck was against her, for by then recruitment for the WAAF and the WRNS had closed, leaving only the ATS, in which she was not interested. She knew that she could be drafted into the ATS, the Women's Land Army or the factories, the last of which filled her with horror.

So she decided to become a Land Girl, and in June 1944, on a two-week holiday from her office job in London, she went to a Volunteer Agricultural Camp in Berkshire, and on the strength of her liking the work, duly applied to join the WLA.

After two interviews and a medical she was accepted, and was told to await further instructions. She decided to leave her office job and go again to the VAC in Berkshire to get some further experience. She was issued with the uniform, which she found quite suitable for the work she did, except for the boots, which nearly killed her feet! She spent weeks with blisters on her heels, and for a while had to wear her walking out (i.e. best) shoes for work.

On 22 October 1944, a warm, sunny day, Joan left home with all her clothing stuffed into a kitbag which her father had purchased for her and felt extremely hot in her unaccustomed clothing. She was billeted in Waltham Cross with a married couple who had one child. It was a comfortable billet which she shared with another Land Girl, who arrived the same day. It was the time of the 'doodle bugs', and the family used to go to the public shelter, leaving the two girls in charge of the house, which they enjoyed, and were never afraid. In Joan's case this was rather surprising given her earlier experience of having her home destroyed by bombing..

Joan Stevens,
Women's Land Army

Her first job was in tomato greenhouses in Waltham Abbey. They were long days, ten to twelve hours during the week and Saturdays until lunchtime. Overtime was compulsory every other weekend, which meant working all day Saturday and Sunday, but at least it meant more money at the end of the week. Even so, it was hard to manage on her wages. After tax and insurance, and paying the hire charge for her bicycle, her basic net wage was £2 2s (£2.10p in today's money), out of which she paid £1.10s (£1.50) for her board and lodging. As they did not receive travel warrants they hitched lifts whenever possible, and sometimes managed to get to the local cinema.

Joan's work covered the complete range of tomato growing from seed sowing to the final harvest, then cleaning the glasshouses with the longest-handled brushes she had ever seen. She also did soil flooding and sterilizing, and even some rat-catching! They were accepted as equals by the conscientious objectors with whom they worked, but the foremen were tyrants, in their opinion.

After some months she got a compassionate posting home because of her mother's ill-health, and from then on she worked in a mobile gang of six doing contract work of up to six weeks at any farm to which they were sent: Romford, Havering, Ockendon or Rainham. Sometimes it meant a journey from home on two buses, or a train, and then by lorry. They did whatever work they were asked to do – hedging and ditching, potato and pea picking, making apple boxes, haymaking and harvesting, tractor driving, mucking out cowsheds,

'We could do with thousands more like you..'

JOIN THE
WOMEN'S LAND ARMY

Apply to NEAREST W·L·A COUNTY OFFICE or to W·L·A HEADQUARTERS 6, CHESHAM STREET, LONDON S.W.1

Issued by the Ministry of Labour and National Service in conjunction with the Ministry of Agriculture.

... and Joan Stevens responded to the call!

spreading manure over the fields, and the whole range of market gardening – seed sowing, hoeing to final pulling. She worked with men who were too old for military service; farmers and their sons who were exempt because they were in a reserved occupation; conscientious objectors; Italian prisoners of war, but never Germans,

Not Joan Stevens, but this WLA girl could have been her... "We did whatever we were asked to do – ditching, potato planing, harvesting, tractor driving ..."

who worked in adjoining fields and were guarded by British soldiers. The most difficult times were in the winter, working in rain, snow or intense cold, when hands and lips were chapped and bleeding for weeks on end.

Joan said, "I coped well with the strenuous work and the long hours, We were, after all, young, mainly in our teens and twenties." She has a variety of memories, some amusing, some exasperating: being serenaded by the Italian prisoners during haymaking as they leaned on their pitchforks whilst the girls did the hard work; being marooned on a haystack whilst the farmer's bull paced around below; being chased across a field by three horses of uncertain temperament; getting caught sunbathing minus shirt during a lunch break by the farmer's wife who spied on them through binoculars for most of the day and told them, before they went home, how many times during the day they had gone into the ditch to relieve themselves; dismantling a smouldering haystack whilst the firemen kept it watered down (there had been a spate of stacks being deliberately set on fire.); a feeling of horror when she washed her hands and saw her skin wrinkling up after spending a day sprinkling salt around mangolds; the amusement they felt each evening after mucking out cowsheds when they entered the carriage of the District Line train at Upminster and all the other passengers promptly moved to other carriages; not quite so amusing was her mother's insistence that she take her working clothes off outside the back door before entering the house!

Minor misdemeanours for which the girls could be rebuked included wearing their hats at the wrong angle or having their dungaree legs rolled up during hot weather! Joan did once get into more serious trouble, which resulted in an official warning from the WLA Headquarters. During a bitterly cold spell in 1945 she was hoeing onion seedlings in a very exposed field. Her nose kept bleeding and by 3 o'clock she decided to give up and leave the farm. She was too scared to go home so went to the cinema in Romford. Ironically, the film was 'For Whom the Bell Tolls'! Her parents never found out.

Eventually, Joan was discharged on medical grounds because of injuries received in falling off a haystack, due to the negligence of the farmer. A Land Army official called at her home to see if she wanted to lodge a complaint against the farmer (which she did not) and in the course of conversation her mother let slip that Joan had had rheumatic fever during childhood. She had not disclosed this at her interview, and her GP had not mentioned it on her medical form. Had it been known, she would not have been allowed to join the WLA.

Like all discharged Land Girls, Joan was offered retraining. She chose a secretarial course which she attended for six months, and from then on did office work. Her only other 'gratuity' was a parcel of clothes consisting of a greatcoat, jodhpurs, thick socks and other items of farm workers' clothing! Having no use for them, Joan sent them back.

While the men and women who had served in the armed forces were awarded medals in recognition of their service, the Land Girls received nothing for their invaluable contribution to the war effort, and it was not until 2005 that they, along with the 'Bevin Boys' and other civilians, were belatedly awarded badges commemorating their service. By this time, of course, many had passed away.

Joan moved around the country for some years after the war, ending up in Derby, where she has lived for the past 43 years.

Working together – tough but vital for the war effort, leaving memories that would last a lifetime…

Margaret Heath

Women's Land Army

Margaret Heath joined the Women's Land Army at the age of seventeen in 1943, not only because she liked animals but also because she fancied herself in the uniform! However, when her uniform arrived she realised that her measurements had been somewhat inaccurate. Everything was far too big, which had the effect of making her look thin, so that people thought she was recovering from a serious illness!

After an interview at Blenheim Palace by the WVS, and having obtained a uniform that fitted, she reported for work at a dairy farm in Oxfordshire where her main job was milking the cows twice a day. Although some cows were still being milked by hand, Margaret used a machine. This was in some ways harder than hand-milking because the buckets were heavier, and lifting them high up to pour the milk into the coolers was strenuous work.

The day started at 6.30 am with the morning milking. Then they had to deliver it by pony and float to the local village and the nearby RAF camp. After lunch there were jobs around the farm, such as feeding the pig, and then they would have to start preparing for the evening milking. They were twelve-hour days, seven days a week, though they could have some time off on Saturday afternoons, but they still had to be back for milking.

The farmhouse stood empty. Margaret and Sheila, the other Land Girl, lived in a cottage with the cowman's parents, while the cowman and his family lived in the other cottage. Conditions were primitive. There was no electricity, and drinking water had to be fetched from a pump in the village. For washing, rainwater was collected in a tank under the house and pumped up when needed.. Every four weeks Margaret would get a weekend off. Sometimes she would go home, and while she was there her father, a practical man who could turn his hand to anything, would repair her shoes. He would accompany her back to the farm, stay the night and go back the next day. Being a railway driver he travelled free. On Saturday nights Margaret and Sheila would cycle to the dance at the RAF camp, a distance of four miles.

Margaret enjoyed working on the land, and continued with it until 1949. After leaving Oxfordshire she returned to Chesterfield and worked at Lockoford Farm, where she met Jack, her future husband. From there she went a farm at Marsden Montgomey, where they had a herd of beautiful Ayrshires. She and Jack married in 1950.

WLA girls … milking twice a day, with twelve-hour days, seven days a week.

Iris Goodall

NAAFI Manager

Everyone who served in the armed forces during the war looks back with gratitude to the women of the Navy, Army and Air Force Institute, more commonly known as the NAAFI. Here they could go to take a break, have a "cup o' char" and a "wad" (i.e. a cake), have a chat with the girl behind the counter, maybe even do a bit of harmless flirting! It was to the NAAFI that they would go for cigarettes, toothpaste, shaving cream, razor blades and other necessities, and also for entertainment. There was always a piano and someone who could play it. The NAAFI girls would also provide a listening ear for men who were homesick and perhaps worried about what was happening to their wives and girlfriends back home, or just in need of a bit of female company.

Iris Goodall was 16 when the war broke out, and at 18 she married a sailor who was serving on minesweepers. This meant he was away from home for long periods. Wanting to make her contribution to the war effort, but not wishing to be too far from her mother who suffered ill health, Iris decided to join the NAAFI. Following an interview in Mansfield, she was accepted as a trainee manager, and after six weeks she was sent to work in Mansfield and then became a manager at Albert Street NAAFI in Newark, which served a depot of the Royal Electrical and Mechanical Engineers (REME), with a Sub-NAAFI at the Osington Hotel in Newark for local RAF bases. Irene was the youngest manager in the area (she had her twenty-first birthday in Newark), and wore an officer's uniform, although the NAAFI organisation was not part of the armed forces.

Buses were few and far between during wartime, and one day Iris and her friend decided to try to hitch a lift into town. Presently an American ambulance pulled up "You can get in," said the driver, "but there's a stiff inside." They had no idea what he was talking about, but soon discovered the meaning of the word "stiff" as they found

Iris Goodhall, NAAFI Manager ... getting ready to serve 'char and wads'.

themselves next to a dead body! They were travelling quite fast, too fast in the opinion of the local constabulary, who decided to chase them. They outran the police car, but the swaying of the ambulance caused the "stiff" to move about alarmingly!

As the preparations for D Day intensified, Iris volunteered to go down to a mansion in Woking, Surrey, from where NAAFI groups from all over the country were sent to different places to serve the vast numbers of troops being assembled for the Normandy invasion. Iris's team were the last to go because their original destination had been blown up. As part of Sherwood Group 'A' Team, they were sent to Bognor Regis, an open NAAFI for troops of all services and nationalities.

Everything possible was done to maintain the morale of the troops as they waited for D Day. One morning Iris was approached by an officer of the Irish 8th Hussars, who wanted to organise a sports day for his men. Iris provided a special cake for the winning team, but unfortunately it was stolen before it could be presented!

Then came the invasion and it suddenly became very quiet as the men went off to face the horrors on the other side of the Channel. Iris was sent back up north and worked in Ripley. In March 1945, now pregnant with her first child, she left the NAAFI. Her son, John, was born on 1st August, two weeks before the surrender of Japan finally brought the war to an end.

... and for my next trick...!

Keith Gould

'Bevin Boy'

Thanks to a blunder on the part of the Government, mining was not classed as a reserved occupation at the start of the war, and thousands of miners were called up for military service. By 1943 the industry had lost some 36,000 men and the country became desperately short of coal. It could not be imported, and a plea for volunteers to work in the mines was largely ignored, so Ernest Bevin, the Minister of Labour, devised a lottery whereby one man in ten was conscripted not into the armed forces but into the mines. They had no choice in the matter, and most who appealed had their cases refused, even those who had come from office jobs and were not physically suited to the heavy and demanding work underground.

At the start of the war, Keith Gould, aged 15, was working at Plowright's, an engineering firm at Brampton, in Chesterfield. When he was 18 he passed his medical for the Royal Navy, but as he was doing essential war work he was not called up. During this time he was in the Home Guard as a member of Plowright's Platoon. One of the firm's managers was platoon commander, and Keith made an amusing comparison between him and the pompous Captain Mainwaring of the 'Dad's Army' TV series! They were often called out in the middle of the night, sometimes to search for downed German airmen, sometimes for no reason at all, and having only one rifle between six men would have stood little chance against an invading German army! It was on on one of these nights on the moors that he had a full view of the horrific sight of Sheffield being bombed.

Then, to his surprise, Keith was called up as a "Bevin Boy". He was sent with seven other lads for six weeks training at Creswell Colliery, in Derbyshire, and on his nineteenth birthday he went underground at Markham No 2 Colliery at Duckmanton, near Chesterfield. He recalls his first time going down in the cage, and the feeling that he was leaving his stomach behind as it plummeted to

Bevin Boys at Creswell (Derbyshire)

Like many others, Keith Gould volunteered for the Royal Navy, but found himself conscripted for coal mining ... and on his nineteenth birthday he joined lads like these at Markham Pit.

the bottom of the shaft! As his background was in engineering he was given a job as a fitter, his role being to repair any machinery that broke down. This put him under considerable pressure. If the machinery was out of action the face workers could not earn money, and made their displeasure very clear, while the deputies, the men in charge, were equally quick to show their anger if things were not fixed quickly. Although the Bevin Boys at first had to put up with a certain amount of ribbing, or even contempt, from the regular miners, they very soon earned their respect if they did their job efficiently.

The working day started at 7 am and often did not finish until 7 pm. They had to take their meal breaks when they could, as there were no set times. They ate their 'snap' in the company of rats and mice who were very quick to sense when food was around, and sometimes they shared it with the pit ponies, who were equally keen to join the feast! (They were still very much in use at the time). It was a dangerous environment. Apart from the possibility of explosions and roof cave-ins, there was the risk of injury in lethal machinery. Keith was involved several times in the rescue of men who had arms trapped in some piece of equipment. An accident caused Keith's hearing to deteriorate and this became dangerous for him as he could not hear when there was a likelihood of roof falls. So for the rest of his time as a miner (he stayed on for 23 years) he worked on the surface. It is ironic that had he not been called up as Bevin Boy it is unlikely he would have gone down the mines in the first place!

Like so many other men who made a vital contribution to the war effort in civilian rather than military roles, the Bevin Boys did not receive the recognition they deserved until many years later. In fact, they were very shabbily treated. They got none of the privileges accorded to men of the armed forces, yet they faced danger of death and injury every working day. No badges or medals were issued to them, and the general public had little awareness of their existence. Indeed, because they wore no uniform they were often assumed to be conscientious objectors or draft dodgers. Unlike forces personnel, they were denied the right to return to their previous jobs, they received no compensation for injuries and no war pensions.

It was not until 1983, the fortieth anniversary of the first ballot into the pits, that their contribution was finally acknowledged in a TV documentary called 'Bevin Boys – Flukes of Fate', featuring one of the most famous 'boys', the actor Sir Brian Rix. Other former 'boys' included comedian Eric Morecambe and international footballer Nat Lofthouse. Sadly, Keith died in August 2013, aged 89.

Stanley Drabble

Military Vehicle Fitter

Stanley well remembers the day war broke out. On Saturday 3 September 1939 he and three other lads went for a week's holiday to Butlins in Skegness. When they arrived they noticed that all the windows on the camp were painted blue, a reminder that war was imminent. The following morning Prime Minister Neville Chamberlain informed the nation that they were now at war with Germany, and the day after that the four lads, disappointed and dejected, were sitting on the bus going home, their holiday over. At the same time they felt a sense of relief. At last the months of tension, as they anxiously awaited the start of the war that everyone knew was going to happen, were over.

Stan was 18, and working as a joiner on a building site in Hucknall, Notts. However, the outbreak of war brought all house building to an end, and Stan was directed by the Ministry of Labour to a series of construction jobs at various locations such as Newton Aerodrome. Finally, he was sent to Leicester to re-train as a motor fitter. It was here that he had a narrow escape when a bomb fell just outside the training centre. Fortunately it fell on the far side of a railway embankment, which shielded the building from the blast. Had it landed on the near side the damage would have been catastrophic.

For the rest of the war Stan worked at the Chilwell Munitions Depot in Beeston, near Nottingham, where during the First World War a massive explosion had killed 134 workers and injured many more. Given the essential nature of the work at Chilwell, it is surprising that there was only one bombing raid. A bomb hit the factory, and the explosion left an engine up in the roof! Such was the veil of secrecy that nobody knew whether anyone had been killed or injured.

This was a vast workshop where military vehicles of every sort – tanks, lorries, cars, motorcycles – were services and repaired. It was

A Crusader tank on the advance through Germany, 1944

under the direction of REME (Royal Electrical and Mechanical Engineers), with civilians working alongside army personnel, women as well as men. Stanley specialised in compressor systems for Crusader tanks. The hours were long, and he had to work seven days a week. From Monday to Thursday he left home at 5.30 in the morning and did not get back until 9.30 pm, and from Friday till Sunday he would be home by 6. He got just one week off a year. Despite the long hours, Stanley enjoyed the camaraderie of the factory.

Although he was doing essential war work, Stanley was told to report for a medical in preparation for being called up into the army. He was sent to see an ear, nose and throat specialist , and was then told he was classified as Grade 4, which meant he was unfit for military service. He never knew why he had failed. He said he felt bad about this, as many of his friends were in the forces, and although white feathers were not handed out to male civilians as in the First World War, a young man not in uniform could be perceived as someone dodging his duty.

The fact is, however, that wars are not won solely by men on the battlefield. Without the support of the engineers back home servicing and maintaining their transport and equipment, they could not have continued to fight. Quite rightly, Stanley felt proud of his contribution to the war effort, and for the rest of his life he felt aggrieved that the tremendous efforts of Britain's factory workers had received so little recognition. Like many others in non-military roles – the 'Bevin Boys' drafted into the coal mines, the Women's Land Army on the farms, the thousands of women who took on the jobs of men drafted into the forces - their vital contribution to ultimate victory was shamefully overlooked for many years.

After the war, Stanley took over his father's newsagent business and continued to work there until he retired.

Violet Newton

Shop Assistant

The following story was emailed to me by Mrs D. Trevis in response to my letter in the local paper. It tells of a miraculous escape during the Sheffield Blitz involving her mother, Violet, and her grandmother Clara Monks, who, with her husband Bill, had a business in Clowne, Derbyshire. Violet's husband Richard was serving in Africa with the Royal Tank Regiment, so Violet was living with her parents and helping in their shop.

They often went to Sheffield "buying in" for the shop, which is what Violet and her mother were doing when the air raid siren went. They were at one of the regular factories they visited for stock, and because they were well known they were invited to go down to the basement with the rest of the staff, as often it was a false alarm. They had two other choices: to run as fast as they could to catch the bus, but carrying parcels would slow them down, or to leave the parcels at the factory and go back the next day to collect them, which would involve two more bus fares. Her mother decided not to go to the basement as they would miss the bus. Her father would be waiting at Clowne to meet them and help carry the parcels, and as they were not on the phone they could not let him know. Also, there might not be any more buses that night and they would be unable to get home.

So they decided to leave the parcels and run as fast as possible to the bus station. The bus was just setting off but the driver stopped when he saw them waving, and let them on. As they drove out of Sheffield they saw incendiary bombs being dropped. This was to cause fires and light up the steel factories in the target area for the main force of bombers. All lights on the bus had to go out and they made their way slowly up the hill out of the city. Without headlights the driver could see nothing so the conductress had to get out and walk in front of the bus. The driver had his window open so that he could hear shouted instructions like "You're going to hit the kerb...you're crossing the centre line." Whenever an incendiary lit up the sky she would jump back on the bus, ring the bell so he knew she was on, and he would put his foot down and go as fast as possible while there was light available. When that died down the conductress would jump off again and continue to walk in front giving instructions to the driver.

Whenever there was a gap between two houses she could see the city blazing away in the valley, much to her distress. It was a horrendous journey, which lasted nearly three hours instead of the usual fifty minutes. Her father, waiting at the bus stop, was nearly out of his mind with worry, having heard that Sheffield was being bombed.

The following day, Violet and her mother went back to Sheffield to collect the parcels. They got off the bus at Pond Street and as they walked towards the factory they saw rows and rows of bodies covered up. When they got to the factory it was just a pile of rubble. It had taken a direct hit through every floor and all the staff who had gone to the basement had been killed. How relieved they were that they had not gone down to the basement. Had they done so, Mrs Trevis would never have been born. They had lost their parcels but they still had their lives.

WARTIME CHILDHOOD

Children must have found it very hard to understand what the war was all about. For some it meant being taken away from their parents and being sent to faraway places to live with complete strangers, who might or might not have treated them kindly. It meant having to carry gas masks and get used to wearing them. It meant fathers and older brothers and sisters going away, often for years on end, sometimes never coming back. It meant hearing the terrifying wail of the air raid siren and rushing to the shelters where they might have to sit for hours on end listening fearfully to the crash of bombs all around them. It meant total darkness at night, with no glimmer of light showing through the dense blackout curtains.

I interviewed nine people who were growing up during the war, and what became obvious was that, with the incredible resilience of children, they managed to have fun even in these ghastly times. Going out at night, although frightening, could be a great game, and all sorts of mischief could be got up to under cover of darkness! Crashed aircraft provided a ready source of souvenir bullets or pieces of shrapnel to be swapped the next day in the playground. When they were not playing they volunteered to collect scrap metal to be recycled as war materials, or helped with the harvest at the local farms. Although some parents tried to protect them from the harsh realities of war, they could follow its progress even in those pre-television days by listening to the news on the radio or watching newsreels in the cinema. Despite the disruptions to their lives, they still went to school, even if only part time, and continued to study and take exams. When victory finally came, they joyfully celebrated with the street parties that their parents organised and eagerly awaited the return of their elders who had been lucky enough to survive.

Just by not allowing the war to crush their spirits, they too had 'done their bit.'

Joan Stevens

Born 1926

When she was 18, Joan volunteered for the Women's Land Army, and her account of that time appears on Page 91. The events described below happened four years earlier.

Joan was an only child, and lived with her parents in Elm Park, Essex. Like most families, they had an Anderson shelter in their garden, but as it was frequently flooded they ceased to use it during a bombing raid. Consequently they had nowhere to shelter during a raid in October 1940. Joan wrote an account of it, which vividly describes the horror of an air raid. I have quoted it verbatim.

"One evening at the end of October we were sitting in the kitchen – I was reading, my mother was heating some milk on the gas cooker. There was an air raid on but there was nowhere else for us to go so we just stayed there. We heard the sound of a German plane and guns were firing at it. My father decided to go into the garden to see where it was and then came in to say it had been hit and was coming down. He went to the front door to check its progress and as it came down it jettisoned its load of bombs and incendiaries. Unfortunately, as my father opened the door, a 2000 lb bomb exploded in front of our house. We did not hear the bomb coming. I remember a roaring sound and everything went dark; a hole appeared in the side and rear walls of our kitchen; my mother screamed and shouted "Won't anyone save us?" (She was constantly reminded of this for many years. My father thought it was a huge joke!)

"My father, who was in the hall, shouted that the kitchen door was stuck and he would have to knock it down. By that time, hot and cold water from the fractured tanks had started pouring through the ceiling. The front door and stairs had been completely blown away. We crawled through the hole into the garden and my father said we would have to go into next door's shelter. We had to negotiate round two incendiaries on the garden path. My mother, in her shocked state, stepped over them and consequently set her nightdress on fire and burned her legs. A huge sheet of flame from igniting gas came through the hole from which we had crawled.

"My father went off to review the situation and eventually came back with a rescue team as, unknown to us, the bomb had fractured the main water pipe in the road and this was cascading everywhere. My mother, who had also been scalded by the hot milk, had to be carried from the shelter. I was dressed only in pyjamas and slippers and by this time walking was difficult against the flow of water. To add to our misery, it had also started to rain.

"The damage to surrounding properties was considerable and the crater extended over two pavements, the road and our front garden right up to the front door. The boulders strewn around seemed enormous. An ambulance was summoned to take my mother to Oldchurch Hospital, Romford. This duly arrived but broke down on the way, and it was two hours before she eventually got to the hospital.

"My father left me in the care of neighbours while he went to a first aid post to get a head wound dressed. Later he found me in a public shelter near Elm Park Station. I was very wet and bedraggled so he borrowed a blanket into which I wrapped myself while he dried my clothes over a paraffin stove.

"In the morning we went to a church in North Street, Hornchurch, which was being used as a reception centre for homeless families. I was given a pair of trousers, a coat (very thin), jumper, shoes and socks. My father was given £10 as an immediate clothing allowance, and £20 for furniture. As we had no home it hardly mattered. After five days we had to leave and my father arranged for us to stay with his two sisters, who also lived in Hornchurch. We slept on the floor for the next two months.

"We had been very worried about our canary, who had been buried under the kitchen debris but was eventually rescued by the demolition squad some three days later. Fortunately he had had sufficient food and water and had sung all day so his exact location was known. The larder door had fallen over his cage and this had sheltered him from the elements and debris which were constantly falling down.

"He had been taken to the home of a PDSA inspector, and a week later my father and I went to collect him. On the way a German plane suddenly flew low over the road and started machine-gunning. My father pushed me to the side of the wall of a house for protection. Having only just been bombed, this was a somewhat unnerving experience."

Beryl Hoole

Born 1934

Beryl's family of thirteen were crammed into a two-up-two-down terraced house on Scarsdale Road, Chesterfield. Although she was only five when the war broke out, she can actually remember Prime Minister Neville Chamberlain's broadcast announcing that we were at war with Germany. She did not understand what it was about, but she could tell from the anxious looks on her parents' faces that it was something serious.

One of her most vivid memories was the sight of hundreds of little tents on the field of the nearby BTH factory, and a lot of soldiers sitting around looking very tired, many with bandages around their heads and arms in slings. These, she learned later, were evacuees from Dunkirk, from whose beaches some 330,000 men had been miraculously rescued as the invading Germans closed in on them. The hospitals were so overwhelmed with casualties that the 'walking wounded' were having to be temporarily accommodated wherever there was space. Eventually, they were moved to more permanent billets. Later in the war she recalls seeing a large number of tanks passing through Chesterfield on their way south as part of the build-up for D-Day.

Another vivid memory was the air raid wardens knocking on the door telling everyone to go to the air raid shelter at Gilbert Heathcote Boys' School. As they waited in the queue for the shelter they could see the vivid red glow in the sky over nearby Sheffield, and searchlights sweeping the sky for enemy bombers which the anti-aircraft guns would attempt to shoot down. Sometimes the bombs fell closer to home, as on the night when the nearby village of Tupton received a stick of bombs which killed some thirteen people and injured many more. Tupton was not the intended target; the pilot was merely jettisoning his bombs so as to escape pursuing British fighters. On another occasion a German plane followed a train along the line to Chesterfield and then proceeded to machine-gun people in the town near Robinson's Works. It is not known how many casualties there were.

For Beryl and her family, everyday life involved adapting to wartime conditions. Everyone had to carry a gas mask, and she recalls her baby niece having a 'carry cot' type which housed the entire child and had to be pumped up. The family ration book was an essential item, and to supplement their meagre food allowance her parents kept rabbits, some of which were for eating and some for pets. Fortunately for the pets, times were never so hard that they had to go into the pot! They also kept hens and had a share in a pig. When it was slaughtered they had pork joints and bacon. An allotment provided a supply of fresh vegetables. There were no freezers in those days, so as much fruit and veg as possible was preserved in Kilner jars or kept cold in the cellar.

Dorothy recalls going to the cinema and watching newsreels giving the latest war news, with pictures of the places where fighting was taking place. She was particularly upset by the pictures of the prisoners released from the concentration camps, who looked like living skeletons.

Holidays were few and far between, and usually spent in Doncaster rather than the Costa Brava! It was more a case of Europe coming to England, with large numbers of Polish refugees and Italian prisoner-of-war in the area, many of whom stayed on after the war. Street parties would be held whenever anyone from the area came back.

Richard Tadman

Born 1932

Though he has lived in Ripley, Derbyshire, since 1988, Richard was born in Maidstone, Kent but moved to Polegate, in Sussex. However, when war broke out his father, believing that they would be safer away from the coast, moved the family to the village of Loose, near Maidstone, where they were actually in greater danger because they were right on the flight path of German bombers on their daily raids on London. This part of Kent became known as 'Hell's Corner', even by the Germans!

Between August and October 1940 the Battle of Britain raged overhead as the Hurricanes and Spitfires of the RAF fought off the massive fleets of Luftwaffe bombers and fighters. At their village school they would spend long periods underground in the air raid shelter, bravely trying to recite their multiplication tables against a background of rattling machine guns and the heavy crump of anti-aircraft gunfire. Four of the oldest boys were always seated near the entrance to dig them out in the event of a bomb falling near the shelter.

After school they would scavenge in the fields, picking up spent bullets and cannon cases and pieces of shrapnel. Prizes souvenirs were the nose caps, which were considered good for bartering for rarer items brought into school. Occasionally they would go on an exciting dash on their heavy old 'sit-up-and-beg' bicycles to the site of a crashed aircraft. It would be guarded by one or two soldiers, who would give them pieces of the aircraft to get rid of them. At other times they would be told in no uncertain terms to leave everything alone as the fuel and bullets were still in a dangerous state.

Like most of the village boys, Richard belonged to the Loose Swiss Scout Troop. The scoutmaster, Jack Barcham Green, was a prominent local businessman in Maidstone. Although having to run is paper manufacturing mill and serve in the Home Guard, he still found time

Richard Tadman age 10-11 in 1942-3, wearing his Scout badge

to organise the scout meetings. He was a firm disciplinarian and a great leader, respected by everyone. He was passionate about boys "doing their bit" for the war effort by collecting waste paper and jam jars on their 'trek cart' (a two-wheeled builders cart) and depositing them at the back of their headquarters for recycling. He would take them on camps and encourage them to help the local farmer with harvesting the corn into stooks, a method that has long since disappeared.

In June 1944, Just as the Allies were landing on the D-Day beaches in Normandy, the Germans began firing the deadly V1 flying bombs. It is commonly believed that they all fell on London, but in fact 2400 fell on Kent, 200 more than on London. This was because some ran out of fuel before they reached their target, while others were shot down by anti-aircraft guns. Some had even been sabotaged by slave workers in the occupied countries, a dangerous practice which meant certain death if they were caught, but it was their only means of hitting back at the hated enemy. The only fighters that were fast enough to catch them were the Meteors, the first jet-propelled aircraft to go into service with the RAF. They would fly alongside the V1s and flip them over with their wings, an effective but dangerous manoeuvre.

Richard writes, "I vividly remember hearing a 'doodle bug' (the popular name for the V1) and the loud rocket engine that sounded like a motor bike without a silencer. When the motor stopped, it meant it was going to dive down and blow up. We were in school at the time and were told by our teacher to hurry up and get under our desks. We did, and waited for the explosion that came a few seconds later. It crashed into a large house a few hundred yards away, which fortunately was empty at the time. Many nearby houses had complete window frames blown out and other structural damage, but amazingly there were no casualties. School finished there and then,

The V1 flying bomb, 'The Doodlebug'

and we were taken by our scoutmaster to help clear up the rubble. When we arrived home our mothers were in a terrible state because most of them had been working in the nearby strawberry fields at the time of the explosion and had been wrongly told that the V1 had blown up the school. Being war-hardened, they soon got over their panic attack!"

Most of the casualties in and around Maidstone were caused by V1s or aircraft jettisoning their bombs to escape pursuing fighters. However, Maidstone was sometimes targeted because of the large railway marshalling yards, factories producing war materials and the barracks of the Royal West Kent Regiment, as well as the nearby Detling airfield. Richard remembers being told to get under the stairs when the air raid sirens sounded.

On one occasion Richard and his fellow scouts were mustered for a St George's Day parade and were told to expect a distinguished visitor. This turned out to be none other than Wing Commander Guy Gibson, hero of the famous 'Dam Busters' raid of May 1942. Sadly, Gibson did not live to see the end of the war. He was killed when his aircraft was shot down over Holland in 1944.

Richard writes of his wartime childhood: "We had no computers or playstations in those days. Our blackberries and apples grew in the orchards, where the twitter was from the birds eating the cherries!. Instead of taking a backpack to school we had to carry our gas mask, which was in a small square box and went everywhere with us. Fortunately they were never needed and eventually we just left them at home."

Charles Binham

Born 1934

Charles, from Derby, was just five when he heard his first air raid siren. "You'll hear a lot more" said his mum, which was probably not very reassuring to a young child. Charles's father was a regular soldier based at Catterick, in North Yorkshire, and Charles lived with his mother and sister near the Rolls Royce factory. As this was a prime target for German bombers, they were evacuated to Chellaston, then on the outskirts of the city, where they lived for 18 months.

In 1941 his father was invalided out of the army, and decided that as Chellaston was getting more bombing raids than Derby they might as well move back to the family home. There they stayed for the rest of the war. Charles only recalls one raid in daylight on the Rolls Royce factory. Later he and his friends found a downed German aircraft on the ground, and eagerly searched for souvenirs to exchange in the playground the next day.

Charles enjoyed helping out at the local farm, milking the cows, picking potatoes or whatever else needed doing. In exchange he would be given a plate of ham, eggs and potatoes, often the equivalent of a week's rations! He also enjoyed growing vegetables and had his own allotment at the age of eleven.

He recalls meeting German prisoners of war out on working parties. Sharing a cup of tea with them, he learned that so far from being monsters they were just ordinary boys not much older than himself, victims of the insanity of war.

Dorothy Walker

Born 1928

Dorothy Walker was born and brought up in Leicester but has lived for many years in Chesterfield. She was kind enough to lent me a copy of her life story "Reminiscences" from which I have quoted extensively in this account.

The war broke out just as Dorothy was about to start her secondary education at Alderman Newton's Girls' School in Leicester. However, the building still had to have sandbag barriers erected around it for protection against air raids, so while this was being done they had to share the buildings of the larger Wyggeston Girls' School in the suburbs. One week they had the building from 8.00 am till 12.15 while Wyggeston occupied it from 12.45 to 5.00 pm, and the following week the times were reversed. As there were no lockers the girls had to carry all their books, PE equipment and domestic science equipment with them, as well as a haversack containing " a half pint flask of water in a metal or wicker cover, an unbreakable cup, packets of dry biscuits, nuts and raisins and glucose barley sugar drops all in a small tin, a two-foot square of mackintosh to sit on and a spare pair of stockings", all ready to be carried down to the underground shelter in the event of an air raid. As if this was not enough they also had to carry a gas mask and a coat or mackintosh. They must have been bent double with the weight of all this equipment!

Dorothy says, "I clearly remember the declaration of war. It was a lovely sunny day, 3 September 1939, and June (my sister) and I were on the garden seat by the open door into the dining room where Mother and Father were listening to the wireless. The Prime Minister Neville Chamberlain's sombre voice came out clearly announcing that Hitler had failed to respond to his ultimatum to suspend the invasion of Poland and that, consequently, "This country is now at war with Germany."

One of the first actions of the government was to evacuate children

Dorothy Walker with her family, 1939-40

from London and other major cities likely to be bombing targets. For children brought up in the slums, it must have felt as though they had been transported to another planet, so different was the environment in which they found themselves. Dorothy's parents were asked to take an evacuee, and it is clear that this child's experience of life was far removed from theirs.

"We had an evacuee for a time, a little boy called Peter. He was about eight years old and came from a very poor family in Mile End. He had never slept in a proper bed until he came to us in need of a thorough bath and hair wash. Despite his grubby background he refused to touch the earth in the garden because it was "dirty" and he would not help pick vegetables, let alone pick off the caterpillars from the cabbages. He could not read or write but could calculate in his head and cheat Mother over the change from errands if he got the chance! After he left, we found under his mattress several receipts for money I had paid in school; he obviously thought they were of value.

"Occasionally, his father would come up in a lorry; he was not in the army and seemed to have both time and petrol. He would take out Peter and his little brother who lived across the road. These 'outings' seemed to consist of father driving round to the local public house where the boys played in the garden. One day, Mother and Father took Peter and June out by bus to Bradgate Park, thinking they would enjoy the space and countryside. Mother was horrified when, as they returned through a narrow city street from the bus station, a street of pubs and fish-and-chip shops, Peter stopped, took a deep breath and said in his broad Cockney accent, "Don't it smell lovely!" Finally, after a time, the father fetched both boys back to London from what had been, to them, an alien environment. Facing the bombs was, apparently, preferable."

Air raids were a nightly terror, especially for those who lived in the cities. As protection, the government issued Anderson shelters, which Dorothy describes thus: "It was a large galvanised iron hoop erected over a pit in the garden and covered with a thick mound of earth and a thick carpet-curtain over the doorway. It was fitted with benches at the sides and a basic supply of first-aid kit and emergency rations, including water. The stirrup pump and bucket of water stood outside ready for a possible incendiary bomb on the house. However, the shelter was prone to condensation and flood and was cold and uncomfortable so that later, when we had longer air raids, we slept under the large wooden dining room table which had been moved to the inner corner of the room where the two houses adjoined. These were reputed to be the safest places and the easiest from which rescuers could dig out casualties in the event of the house collapsing. Fortunately it never came to that."

She described the fear that the sound of approaching bombers caused. "The wailing of the sirens...was a frightening sound and we would seize gas masks, clothes and, if we were not already bedded down, scurry to our 'shelter'. Leicester did suffer bombing raids but none on the severity of Coventry. I remember standing on our front porch on several occasions and seeing the glow in the sky, lit up by the fires in Coventry some thirty miles away."

Keeping the nation fed at a time when importing food had become almost impossible was a major priority for the government, and rationing was another fact of wartime life with which the civilian population had to cope. "At first it was just basic foods; later, clothes and other goods were added. Everyone was issued with a ration book with coupons which had to be cut out or stamped to cancel them. Sometimes even the basics were not easily come by as shops "ran out" so queuing became essential. Goods such as oranges, which were imported, virtually disappeared as all shipping space was needed for

Dorothy Walker (left) helping with the harvest, 1941

the war effort. At one time the *weekly* ration per person was: 4 ounces (oz) bacon, 8 oz sugar, 2 oz tea, 2 oz butter, 1 oz cheese, 4 oz margarine, 1/10d (a shilling and ten pence) worth of meat and one egg a fortnight. Manual workers had a slightly larger allocation of cheese, etc. Eggs were in short supply and a powdered, dried-egg mixture was issued every other month. The ration books contained additional coupons known as 'points'. These could be used for 'extras', not on the normal ration, such as dried and canned fruit when they were available. There was a rather strange canned fish called 'snoek', rather like tuna. Occasionally there were jams, said to be made of turnips, and other 'ersatz' foods such as marrow disguised as melon."

To supplement their rations people kept livestock. "Mr Lord next door began to keep hens and, when he was away on ARP duty and Mrs Lord couldn't cope, Mother looked after them. He had a vicious cockerel, so he lent Mother his wicket-keeping pads and gloves to protect her when she entered the enclosure. As Mr Lord was a big man and Mother was small she looked rather overwhelmed! In return we were given eggs which Mother preserved in a bucket of isinglass. It was all horrible and slimy to take one out.

"People also collaborated in creating co-operatives such as 'pig clubs'. Permission would be given for someone to rear a pig and members would help and also provide swill from any food waste.

Then, when the time came for slaughter, they would draw lots for the particular cut which was their allocation of meat."

Like millions of others, Dorothy's family 'dug for victory' by turning their gardens into allotments. "Father dug up our entire lawn early in the war to extend the vegetable patch so that we were largely self-sufficient in potatoes, carrots and greens in season." Harvesting also became a communal effort, with school children being roped in to 'do their bit'. "We were taken by lorry for days out to local farms to help with pea-picking and, less enjoyably, potato-picking, in the days before fully mechanised harvesting, of course. It entailed bending down to sift the potatoes from the loosened earth and putting them on carts. It was backbreaking, cold and, usually, muddy and wet work.

"More enjoyable, though equally hard work, were harvest camps. Every summer holidays our teachers took a large group of us to Kibworth Beauchamp for some weeks. We lived in the school there, sleeping on straw palliasses set round the school hall, taking it in turns to do the cooking, and travelling out to farms every day to help with the harvest. We worked on government farms with large fields of flax as well as corn. Flax was harvested by workers bending down and working backwards round the field, pulling the flax, making it into soft sheaves ready for loading onto carts. Like potato picking, it was backbreaking."

It was quite normal for prisoners-of-war to be employed on farms. "We were helped on the farm by German and Italian prisoners-of-war who were brought by guards from the prison camp each day. The Italians were charming and would sing as they worked, but the Germans were more serious and harder working. All were co-operative and polite, though. They were probably pleased to be out of the camp and, indeed, out of the fighting at the front."

As well as farm work, Dorothy also helped with the Christmas post. "Because of conscription, there was a shortage of post office staff at busy periods. We had to get up very early indeed on dark winter's mornings, face the blackout and travel by tram to the sorting office...We were sent out on delivery rounds with heavy mailbags, usually to parts of the city which we did not know."

Clothing was also rationed, and much ingenuity went into clothes made from recycled material. "Father managed to salvage some old maps about to be discarded from the office. These were printed on a fine linen-cotton background so we boiled them in the copper and then used the material for petticoats and blouses. I still have a very fine handkerchief made from the cut-offs. Discarded parachutes, which were occasionally available, were also excellent for being made into nightdresses and underwear. Once the war was over, blackout curtains were recyclable, especially as clothes rationing continued until 1949."

Dorothy Walker at Girl Guide Camp, 1946

Dorothy was a keen member of the Girl Guides and later became a lieutenant. On one occasion she was the quartermaster for the annual camp, organising all the rations. "So that I could provide a meal fairly quickly I bought enough fish for thirty of us and cooked it at home, ready to be heated up when we arrived. We were camping near Swithland Woods. Unfortunately there had been tremendous storms earlier and we found the campsite, on its rocky hill, was under water so we all had to return home. The Guides were whisked home by lorry before I could share the fish out amongst them, so my task was to go along our street asking the neighbours if they could use some cooked fish, wartime restrictions making it impossible to contemplate throwing it away! Most of the neighbours were delighted."

By 1944 the end of the war was in sight. Dorothy and her fellow-guides were at camp at Woodhouse Eaves on D Day. "It was gloriously sunny and all day we watched the planes and gliders from the nearby American and British air bases flying over, carrying parachutists and their equipment." However, the end of hostilities did not mean and end to war work. "When I was at university, though I did not run a Guide company then, a group of us were asked to take a company of girls to camp in Devon. They came from an area of

*Dorothy
Walker's
ID Card,
for 'Boys
and Girls
under 16
years'*

Coventry that had been bombed so this was a holiday to take them away from the devastation and, perhaps, help them get over the trauma. Our job was to cope with all the work in setting up the camp, collecting wood, cooking, etc. while they were taken down to the beach or further afield on outings. In a way it was a kind of war service for us."

1945 was the end not only of the war but also of Dorothy's schooldays. Having gained her Higher School Certificate (the equivalent of today's A Levels), she went on to read English at Nottingham University, followed by a one-year PGCE teacher training course. There followed a highly successful career which saw her rise to become head of the prestigious Netherthorpe Grammar School in Chesterfield, the first woman to occupy that post in its 400-year history!

Valerie Revill

Born 1938

One of the saddest situations for men who served overseas during the war was that when they came home their children did not know them. They left them as babies who had no memory of them, and returned as complete strangers. This often caused resentment; children who had got used to living in all-female households suddenly found a man whom they had never met had taken over as head of the household.

This was the situation faced by Valerie Revill, from Sheffield. Her father, a former regular soldier before the war, was recalled for war service and posted overseas, and he did not come back until Valerie was seven. These are her memories of her wartime childhood.

"My mother was a dressmaker, and we lived with my paternal grandmother. I remember seeing my mother through a perspex rectangle. These were for babies until they graduated to Mickey Mouse gas masks. It was years later that I saw an exhibition of war memorabilia and realised that these canvas bags with the perspex window were for young babies. I remember starting school at the age of four with my Mickey Mouse gas mask.

"There were very few men about in those days – mostly older men or those in essential occupations. I can remember women digging out the ground for air raid shelters. They turned their hands to everything, growing vegetables, driving trams and working in factories while grans looked after the children. How they coped I don't know. Certainly few of today's young women could turn their hands to the many jobs women took over.

"My mother volunteered for the steel works and operated a milling machine, while still sewing at night and at weekends. She made many winter coats out of blankets for local women. I remember years later, when I did a stint as an Industrial Nurse, seeing a milling machine. It was filthy, running with oil and grease, and the noise was horrendous. It was massive. I could hardly believe my mother had worked on a machine like this. In fact the factory was like Dante's Inferno. The management were aghast at my per-ception of the horrible conditions. "It is the cleanest factory in Europe", they said!

"We lived on the east side of Sheffield where virtually all the steel works were situated, alongside the River Don, and they were a prime target for German bombers. Some-times they made mistakes in their raids, fooled by the many rivers. On one raid they followed the River Sheaf by mistake and bombed the city centre. One pub was flattened, the Marples I think. There were no survivors. C and A's department store was also destroyed. There were frequent air raids but I only remember going to the shelter once and there was water up to my knees. From then on we went down into the cellar. I remember the anti-aircraft gun emplacements on the hillside overlooking the houses and the factories. Generally it was older men who operated these.

"I remember VE Day, as Hitler was strung from my bedroom window over a bonfire! Then my father came back, very thin and unkempt, with a big beard. Of course I did not know this stranger and was very resentful towards him. I feel so sad that this probably happened to many men returning from war. I think I was in my teens before I realised what a great guy he was, and years later I found out why he was so thin. He had been giving his food and whatever he could scrounge to other foreign women with children. He never said this to me or Mum, but I overheard him telling a friend – that all he could see was his own wife and me as a babe in arms."

How sad it must have been for Valerie's father, nursing through all those heart-breaking years of separation the dream of being reunited with his little daughter, only to be greeted with hostility on his return. At least for him there eventually came reconciliation; many others were not so lucky, and the scars of those years of separation never healed. In fact the relationship became even closer some years later. When her husband died at the age of 48 of a brain haemorrhage, he became a substitute father for Valerie's children. Valerie now lives in Belper.

Joan Fowler

Born 1936

Joan was very young when she first encountered the brutal realities of war. She was just four when, on the night of 30 September 1940 an unexploded bomb lodged itself right outside her pantry window. She was carried in the arms of an ARP warden to his house, where she was provided with boys' clothes to wear, much to her dismay! She was then sent to stay with relations in Langley.

Being so young at the time her memories of the war are vague. She recalls getting her sweet ration on Sundays, the milk being delivered by horse and cart, and of course the blackout. She also recalls the air raid shelter in her school, and evacuees arriving from Birmingham, one of whom was billeted with her aunt.

She met her future husband at the Miners' Holiday Camp in Skegness in 1950, when she was 14. Two years later she went back again and they were reunited, and eventually married.

Courtesy of www.picturethepast.org.uk

Fun at the Derbyshire Miners' Holiday Camp at Skegness in the 1940s-50s

Audrey

Age Unknown

Audrey emailed this account of her wartime childhood in response to my letter in the local paper but did not wish to be interviewed.

"I was evacuated with my elder sister from Rainham (a small village then) to, of all places, Deal, Kent, where we got the very first air raid. The area called Hell's Corner was a direct route to London. Any bombs they hadn't dropped on London we got on their way back to Germany. I can remember this well as we were playing on the beach when this strange loud noise started and someone grabbed hold of me and took me into the castle where everyone was heading.

"We were only there a short while when we were moved to another house as the women we were with thought we were too fussy as we weren't used to a tin bath in front of the fire, as we had a bathroom at home and we didn't have one at hers.

"The house we were moved to was multi-storey and housed a lot of adults from the forces. This only lasted a short while as my mother fetched us back saying if we were going to die then we would all die together.

"I can remember that to begin with we spent every evening in an air raid shelter built of brick, as we had a raid every night. In the end they just left the warning on permanently night and day. After a couple of weeks we slept indoors. I can remember night after night sitting on the very large window seat watching doodle bugs, searchlights, planes dropping their bombs and my mother praying. We also saw what they called flaming onions in the sky. We lived about a quarter of a mile from where they used to fire big guns and they used to rock the house when they went off.. When it happened during the day my friend and I used to go and collect shrapnel from the road in front of our homes, but not until it had cooled down. I remember having loads of it. I can remember schools closing down for a while.

"Sometimes during air raids my mother took the three of us into the cupboard below the stairs and one day a bomb dropped nearby, and the door slammed shut. We all had to shout and bang until our next door neighbour came and released us, as in those days there was no need to lock your doors for security.

"We never wanted for food items as we lived next to orchards and in return for fruit, eggs etc. my mother allowed the farmer's sister to have a weekly bath. My mother worked as a cashier in the local Co-op butchers, so meat was plentiful too.

"I can remember hearing adults speak of people shopping and having part of their clothing blown off with the blast from bombs. Our next door neighbours had an incendiary bomb in their garden, which made a fairly large hole. I was once knocked to the floor from the blast of a bomb dropping nearby, but felt nothing."

May Matthews

Born 1931

May was born in Arnold, then a village on the outskirts of Nottingham but now a suburb of the city, and she was eight years old when the war broke out. When she was eighty she was asked to give a talk to the children at her local primary school about her wartime childhood. With amazing clarity she recalled the experience of being an ordinary child during those extraordinary years. I have drawn extensively from her notes in writing her story.

She began by comparing her life as a child with that of today's children. "You get up to go to school and there is a huge choice of what you can eat for breakfast, the house is warm and you have the use of a bathroom. In September 1939 only a few houses had bathrooms, and most toilets were outside in the garden. There was no central heating, so most houses were very cold in winter. It was normal to wake up and see thick patters of frost on the inside of the windows. They were beautiful, and different every day, but the icy air in the room made it hard to get out of bed. Most houses only had a cold water tap, and that was where four or more children had to wash. Many boys and girls had chilblains, painful swellings on their hands and feet, because of the cold.

"Today's children get taken to school by car or bus. In those days we walked, in my case a mile each way. The only transport was the farmer's dog cart bringing children from the outlying farms. There were no school dinners. Everyone walked home at 12 and returned to school at 1.45, so four journeys were made each day. Cars were a very rare sight. Only the doctor had one, and there was one in the police station. Nobody had a telephone, not even the school. Only the doctor and the police station had one.

" It would be hard for you to imagine how quiet it was in those times. No noisy washing machines, no vacuum cleaners, no food mixers. Some houses were even without electricity and still used gas lamps, like the street lights. Horses and carts were used for delivering goods, with just an occasional lorry or bus on the main road to town."

It did not take long for May to become aware of the war. One day she was going into school, happily chatting to her friends. "Suddenly we heard the sound of an aeroplane engine, and at once the teacher called out "Get in the doorway, quick!" and we were pushed and bustled into a doorway set back from the pavement. The teacher was frightened, and we were all upset. Then, as the plane droned away, she explained her strange action. "Don't you know we are at WAR?" I didn't want to ask what she meant, for fear of looking foolish, and waited until I arrived home before asking what war was. Reluctantly, it was explained to me that another country wanted to fight us, and life was going to change. I remember thinking that I didn't want to fight anyone. However, what I had been told was true. Life did change for us that day, sometimes frightening, other times exciting, often difficult, but I grew up to feel part of the struggle everyone would share.

"Suddenly there were new things to learn, like air raid practice. All the windows had to have sticky tape criss-crossed on them to stop flying glass. Then we watched as workmen took down signs over shops that told the name of the place. All the signposts were collected in the council cart and the old horse pulled them away.

"Then there was the blackout. Everyone had to buy yards of dense black material to make curtains for windows and doors. All the shops had curtains behind the doors so no light escaped. The few vehicles on the roads had masks over their headlights. Many people were knocked down during those first months. I had been in a shop with my aunt and when we came out into the dark night I walked straight into a lamp post. The next day I had a black eye and a huge egg-shaped swelling on my forehead!

At first children were not allowed to go out and play as parents were worried in case there was an air raid. It took some time for shelters to be built. Men dug holes ready for their shelters, and huge mounds of earth started appearing in gardens. If there was even a small space left it would be dug up and planted with vegetables. Many remembered the 1914-18 war and how difficult it could become. Tinned food was put away in boxes and stored in a dry place. There were no such things as sell-by dates then!

"We didn't have a shelter but we had a deep cellar. Candles were stored down there, as were garden chairs. As my mother had not been well I had gone to live with my aunt and uncle, where there was an older cousin and another aunt. So when an army officer came to the house to see if we could have a soldier billeted with us, he decided we did not have the room. I was disappointed. I thought it would be fun to have a soldier in the house, but my aunt and uncle were relieved."

During the First World War, poison gas had been used in the trenches, and its effects were horrific. It turned to liquid in the lungs and the victim choked to death. There was a very real fear that in this war it would be used against civilians, so everyone was equipped with a gas mask, even babies. For May putting it on was a most unpleasant experience.

"I remember when I had to be fitted with a gas mask. We went into a large building with a lot of other families. As soon as we entered the hall I was overcome by a horrid smell of rubber. I wanted to leave at once, but a man pointed to a bench and told us to wait our turn. All too soon the awful mask was taken from a box, smelling stronger than ever now it was so close. As someone pulled it up over my face I dared not breathe. So off it came and I was told to try again and this time not to take a deep breath. What a performance! I was hot and still hated the rubber smell. Babies screamed as they were put into big bag-like masks, their mothers almost in tears as they were taught how to use the pump to keep them alive. Small children ran around in funny-coloured masks, hiding behind the piles of boxes as they waited for other family members to be fitted.

"At last we were free to go, but we were told that from now on the gas mask had to be with us at all times. It was most uncomfortable. The cord pulled on my shoulder and the hard box banged its corners on my body. We kept them by our desks in the classroom and took them out with us at playtime. Every so often the teacher would say "Take out your masks and put them on." She would time us and we would have to be as quick as possible. The we would have to carry on with our classwork still wearing our masks so as to get used to them. After a while the rubber smell faded and the hard boxes were replaced by cases of soft material, some made by our mothers."

Air raid practice was another regular activity. As the school did not at first have shelters, other arrange-ments had to be made. "Once outside, everyone had to run as fast as possible to the house of a friend or relative, or of someone who was home in the day. Very few homes had shelters at the time, but it meant that if a bomb fell on any of the houses perhaps only a few children might be killed whereas if one hit the school when it was full of children the casualty rate would be horrific. As a further precaution, half the children would go to school in the mornings and half in the afternoons, so as to reduce the number of children on the premises at any one time.

"When the school shelters were completed and we went inside for the first time, it was rather awful. It was dark and felt damp and fusty. There was a wooden bench along one wall, and that, too, was damp. No one wanted to go into the gloom, but eventually we were all seated with our backs to the glistening wall. There was some very low blue lighting which did nothing to cheer us, and we had some candles for emergency use. The teachers did their best to lift our spirits. We sang songs, then had a story, but it was a very subdued group of children that made their way out when the 'all clear' sounded. Fortunately we did not have the heavy air raids that some cities suffered, but one dreadful morning we arrived at school after a night raid to find both staff and children in tears. We had heard a bomb drop close by, just one, but it had hit our teacher's house and she had died. It made us realise that all the new rules we had to live by were for a serious reason and we had better take note."

For most of the time during the war, everyday life went on in May's village just as in peacetime, but every so often the war would dramatically intrude into their lives. One summer's day May and her best friend were walking back to school after lunch, chatting happily, when suddenly they heard the sound of an aircraft. "Then, as the noise grew louder, we looked up into the clear blue sky and saw a Spitfire almost overhead. Only then did we become aware of another noise, like a distant rattle, and we saw another plane. Within seconds they were chasing each other across the sky. We said "Oh, it must be a dogfight." We had heard of these air battles but had never seen one. Almost immediately the fighters swooped down low. The rattling

May Matthews, Easter 1941, age 10, with a child who was looked after by her family during the war.

was deafening and seemed to be happening all around us. As we stood astonished on the pavement, a door opened and a woman leaned out, grabbed us both and pulled us into her house. It was all over in seconds, and after a few minutes the woman opened her door and told us to run as fast as we could to school just a few hundred yards away. As we ran the sirens wailed out but the planes had gone, leaving behind two shaken little girls and hundreds of machine gun bullets that had hit the road, sheds and roofs on that previously quiet summer's day.

"It may seem strange but although we had talked about dogfights we had not really understood about the bullets. It had never entered our heads that they could bounce off buildings or spray over people. You have to remember that in 1940 we had never seen action pictures of war. There was no television, and newspapers were kept out of children's hands. As far as possible our parents tried to protect us from the war. Talk of death and fighting were avoided when children were in earshot. I think there was a feeling that everyone had to give the young ones a chance to enjoy their early years as much as possible while they could."

One way in which parents in peacetime would have given their children a treat was to take them to the seaside, but in wartime this was impossible, as the beaches were all barricaded off and mined. So the beaches were brought to them. May described the 'Holidays at Home' scheme that local councils organised. "Tons of sand were brought to our local park and a fun fair was set up with puppet shows and entertainers. There were lots of organised games and races. The park would be full of people, many bringing picnics on sunny days. This meant a great deal to us, because it was a place to go and meet friends during the long summer holidays, and there would be new events each week. It meant our parents did not have to worry about us, as there were shelters nearby in case there was an air raid."

However, the serious business of war was never very far away, and May and her friends gradually realised how important it was to 'do their bit' for the war effort. "As we grew older we were able to help more, and this was always fun because we were doing things with our friends. There were many local organisations we could join. I started off in the Brownies and we knitted small garments for the men in the forces. Later, in the Guides, we learned First Aid and some of us helped in the hospitals. We rolled bandages, helped in the kitchens, ran errands for war wounded patients, posted their letters, and when old enough made beds and fetched and carried on the wards. Boys could join the Scouts, the Boys' Brigade or the Army or Air Cadets. They acted as messengers for the Air Raid Wardens, using their bicycles, and collected waste paper and scrap metal for recycling. Every autumn we would have two weeks off school to help with the potato harvest. This was hard work but we got out into the country with friends and there was always much laughter.

"We also joined in with the local adult evening entertainment shows that were put on every month or so. We took part in sketches, sang songs, and many children could play an instrument, as there were a lot of bands in the area. And many homes had a piano. One of our school friends could play the accordion, and one year a group of us went carol singing. It was a great success, and the money went towards buying a Spitfire.

"There was always a target for the school or village to raise money for something like a ship or aeroplane. Our school had adopted a ship, and we sometimes had visits from the crew. We wrote to the sailors and sent parcels containing extra 'goodies'. It was always a special day when we had a visit, and we followed their progress as much as we were allowed to know. At our senior school the geography teacher had a large map of the world on the wall. Every morning she would ask the girls if they knew where their fathers were. She would then place pins in the map indicating their locations. This gave us a better idea of what was happening, as well as improving our knowledge of maps."

Finally, after nearly six long years, the war came to an end and it was time to celebrate. "Most streets had a party, with tables brought out from the houses and lined up in the road. Precious tins of food, saved for years, were at last opened to provide a special treat. A lot of trouble was taken to make things look festive. Garlands were made and bits of material were cut up to string across from house to house for bunting. Later in the evening there was dancing in the park. The crowds were so thick that there was hardly any room to move and the bands played on long after midnight. I could hear them in the distance as I snuggled down to sleep, safe at last in the knowledge that the sirens were never going to wail again."

May Matthews' Post-war Life

The end of the war was greeted with euphoria and rejoicing. Now people no longer had to live in fear of air raids. The lights could burn brightly again as blackout curtains were taken down and gas masks thrown to the far corners of lofts. Soon the menfolk from whom the women and children had been anxiously separated for so long would be coming safely home. However, hard times lay ahead. As the country struggled to get on its feet again, there would be several years of austerity. Rationing did not end; in fact it became even more severe than during the war. The fighting may have finished but the struggle to survive was as hard as ever.

May Matthews, who earlier described her life as a wartime child, was fourteen when the war ended. She has written very eloquently of life during the post-war period, which, despite the hardships, was a time when she experienced the first feelings of attraction towards the opposite sex as she journeyed from childhood to maturity. She begins by describing the joyous celebrations that greeted the end of the war.

"There was such relief and partying, just everyone seemed to be celebrating, as indeed I was myself. Feeling very grown-up and being allowed to join in with the adults after dark, dancing in the park. I had never been out so late alone, although I had to leave long before the music ended. It was like being in a dream, there were lights on everywhere as I ran down the hill to my house. Even as I snuggled up in bed I could still hear the familiar tunes as I drifted off to sleep, imagining I was there among the pressing crowd of dancers, immersed in the most wonderful, powerful, joyous atmosphere I had ever known."

However, euphoria soon gave way to harsh reality.

"Immediately after the war, little changed, in fact shortages became even worse. Food rations were reduced and the importance of growing as much as possible at home was still vital. These

May Matthews, left, age 16 years in June 1947, on a day trip by train to London.

restrictions were hard to manage as everyone was war-weary and hopes for better times were heightened as the fighting ceased. Many adults remembered the previous conflict and how many years it took to recover. Even in 1953, when I got married, sugar and meat were still on ration and sweets had only just come off.

"I think people realised what a long period of strain they had suffered. Everything seemed a bit flat. To end the war had been such a passion and now there was an emptiness bringing other worries. There had been no house building for years. Everything had been for the war effort. Factories had been converted to war production and although this had been done quickly in 1939, now it took a long time to change back. Men couldn't take up their old employment immediately, some never did, buildings had been destroyed and trades changed."

As if there was not enough hardship at this time, one of the worst winters of the century struck them in 1946-47.

"It was so bad it took everyone's energy just to keep going from day to day. All thoughts of building a new future were put on hold whilst we tried to cope with keeping warm and fed. Because of the depths of snow, fuel deliveries could not be made, the coal heaps remained frozen in the pit yards and vegetables froze in the clamps on the farms."

However, with the resilience of youth, May managed to find fun and enjoyment in these hard times.

"For me, swinging between childhood and trying to feel grown up, it was a wonderful time. The Old University Building (she was attending a teacher training course in Nottingham at this time) had some bomb damage and windows in some areas had not been repaired. We sat for a time in coats and gloves, but when the very poor heating system ran out we suddenly found ourselves with an unexpected holiday. Like others of my age we were quickly mobilised for shopping, and in the mornings we would gather with our sledges to call on neighbours and go down the village to collect their supplies. On our return there would be coal buckets to fill and sticks to chop. We would try to harvest some vegetables from people's gardens without pulling them to bits in the fight with the frosted ground. We made a sledge run down the hill, and soon the word went round of the fun we were having. The numbers grew, with younger children being supervised by older ones, for during the war they had often been left in charge while parents were working, fire-watching or doing their bit in the Home Guard."

This was the time when May felt the first stirrings of romance. An older boy asked if she was going to be at the slide that evening, and to her delight she gained permission to stay out after dark, albeit with strict instructions as to what time she came home.

"The slide in the glimmer of the gas lamps looked menacing. It was the first time we fourteen to sixteen year olds had been allowed out that late. The sixteen to eighteen year olds were having great fun. For some of them it was the last fling before being called up for National Service. The boy I had hoped to see joined us. He asked me if I was warm enough and would I like to wear his hat. Would I?? Oh what magic was working that starlit night! The hat was his mother's, a lady's flying helmet, creamy white soft leather with a furry lining, a beautiful thing. I felt transported to another age. However, it was not the start of a lifetime romance and in later years I realised he had not wanted to wear a feminine looking garment in front of older boys anyway!"

Unlike today's ultra fashion conscious teenagers, May's generation had to 'make do and mend' when it came to clothes.

"Clothing was very drab, and even coloured fabric was unobtainable. Many people had long since used up every scrap of saved material. I remember being highly delighted with a hand knitted jumper as my main eighteenth birthday present."

The end of the 40s saw a surge in building to overcome the chronic post-war housing shortage.

"Our wonderful adventure playing field was quickly covered with smart houses and our village changed as the Labour council built a record number of homes, overwhelming the fairly small community where most of the families were known to us, and often related."

The invention of the atomic bomb had brought the war to an end, but now the possibility of nuclear annihilation cast a new shadow over the world.

"Although there was huge relief that we had won the battle, there was a lot of background concern about the atomic bomb. If the subject was broached a cloud would pass over people's faces. Some tried to say they never thought about it but deep down it would not go away. Everyone knew about the red button and how at the end of the day it depended on a few people's decision. So the war's ending was not all glory and peace; we had a different challenge to face."

May has no regrets about growing up during these hard times; on the contrary, she feels it was a privilege.

"I am sure I was very fortunate to grow up in a time of shortages and austerity as I absorbed the way of helping out in any way I could. This did not mean I turned into a 'do-gooder', it was amongst my generation the normal way to behave. A lot was expected of us and yet we had a strange freedom, adults being so very hard-working, often with evening work as well as long days. We were asked to do many jobs to help out. Most of my friends could cook simple things and prepare fruit and vegetables for a meal. We helped out with gardening and looking after chickens and pigs, which gave us a sense of responsibility. By the time we got married we knew a lot about how to cook and look after a home.

"I was proud to belong to the generation that lived through wartime. It gave us a strength and confidence that we could cope whatever, and a knowledge of the importance of family and loved ones, and of enjoying a life that is free."

Reading May's account of her teenage years, one cannot help but reflect on the contrast with the lives of today's young people. Gone is the joyous innocence of those years, to be replaced by the shallow sophistication of a culture where clothes, music and mobile phones are essential. May's generation were brought up to accept responsibility and help others; today, life is all about instant self-gratification. In those days young people learned domestic skills that would stand them in good stead for life; today they scarcely know how to boil an egg. One has to wonder how much better off we are seven decades on from the post-war years. Immeasurably better off materially, but happier? I doubt it.

NATIONAL SERVICE

The war continued to affect people's lives for many years after it had ended. One way in which it did so was through National Service.

The post-war government was determined that Britain was never again to be in such a state of unreadiness for war as it was in 1939, and decreed that all men aged 18 or over, unless medically unfit or in reserved occupations such as farming or mining, were to serve for two years in the armed forces. Those who were going through education or training could have their service deferred, but few got away with it, though many tried.

Retrospective views of National Service vary. Some regarded it as a complete waste of two years, an unwanted interruption to their careers; others found it a formative, beneficial experience, which taught them self-confidence and offered opportunities and experiences that they might never have otherwise had. If nothing else it enabled some of them, in the age before mass tourism, to visit faraway countries which few of their contemporaries had ever seen. Admittedly this was on Her Majesty's Service rather than on holiday, but there were usually opportunities to visit the tourist areas of the country where they were stationed. A very small number saw active service in war zones such as Korea, Malaya and Suez.

In a way the whole *raison d'être* of national Service was obsolete before it started. The invention of nuclear weapons had rendered the possibility of a 1940 style invasion of the British Isles highly unlikely and the consequent need of a large trained defensive force unnecessary. The pressure to end National Service came, in fact, not from the general public but from the service chiefs, who wanted professional, committed volunteers in their ranks, not recalcitrant conscripts. It came to an end in 1960.

Interestingly, this was the start of a new era, in which the younger generation began to rebel against the values and attitudes of their elders. The word "teenager" came into the language, signifying an age group who wore their hair long, had their own fashions and music, and indulged in sex, drugs and rock'n'roll! The last thing they were interested in was military service. The older generation, despairing at what they saw as utterly degenerate behaviour, called for the reintroduction of National Service as a way of instilling some discipline and respect for authority in the young. However, it was not to be, and National Service in Britain passed into history.

Richard Tadman's National Service

Richard's recollections of his wartime childhood appear elsewhere. When he was 20, he was called up for National Service. One day in 1951 a letter arrived, informing him that he was to attend a medical examination at the local snooker hall. He duly did so, and was passed as A1. He was then asked what branch of the armed forces he would like to serve in, and he chose the Navy. However, this would require him to sign on for extended service beyond the compulsory two years, so he chose the army instead. His next decision was whether or not to join the infantry, and as this did not appeal he suggested a tank regiment. This appeared to be a good answer and he was enlisted into the Royal Armoured Corps.

However, it would be some time before he even saw a tank, because he had first to do his basic training, usually referred to as 'square bashing'. He was sent a travel warrant and told to report to Catterick Camp in Yorkshire. Having grown up in rural Kent, he had barely heard of Yorkshire, let alone Catterick. Richard describes the experience of arriving in his own words:

"Eventually arriving in Catterick Camp I, with numerous other fresh-faced, suited and booted young men were greeted by a smart-looking sergeant who informed us that "You 'orrible little men are in the army now and we are going to make soldiers of you!" We then started our basic training, the army's way of making us tough, fearless soldiers (well, sort of!). We did without doubt learn the hard way what discipline really was. Even the streetwise kids soon lost their city swagger; this was achieved in a way only the British Army knew. 'Do as you are told and we will get on alright' was the lesson we learned."

They were then kitted out by the Quartermaster Sergeant with battledress uniforms and other clothing, all khaki, plus black boots, navy berets and numerous pieces of webbing equipment. The sergeant then informed them that they now held the rank of Trooper in the

Royal Armoured Corps, and they were issues with an army number and pay books. They had now lost their civilian identity. As if to emphasise this tey were given the obligatory 'short back and sides' haircut and shown to the huts that were to be their home for the next eight weeks.

Their transformation from civilians to soldiers was in the hands of junior NCOs, and lance corporals in particular. Of one, Richard says: "He seemed semi-human in his attitude to us. These individuals were often short in body size and noticeably so in brain size, due, it

Trooper Richard Tadman age 20 in 17/21 Lancers, at York Barracks Munster, 1952

was said, to being dropped on their heads at birth...We were once told by a lance corporal that we were "naughty 'orrible little men." We never did know why we were naughty or 'orrible, but we were told to parade in our off-duty time outside our huts with our eating irons. Having just had our tea we thought this a strange request, even thinking we might be going to a party! However, we soon found out the reason. We were told to get down on our hands and knees and start cutting the grass outside our hut. "Where are the shears?" we thought, but were promptly told to use our knives, and so about twenty of us started hacking at the blades of grass until we had satisfied the lance-corporal's twisted sense of humour and allowed to go back in and not be 'naughty' again. We even thought we were perhaps being trained for the Ghurkhas, and were being assessed for our skills with a table knife!"

When they were considered safe to be allowed onto a tank gunnery range, they were taken to Warcop, in Cumbria, a more easy-going camp and a pleasant change from Catterick. "We were instructed in the use of the tank's 17-pounder gun, firing at the remains of well-holed tanks situated on the hillsides. When firing ceased, we were taken to see the result of our shooting, and were amazed to see so many holes in the tank's armour. Our confidence was slightly shaken as we had been led to believe that with all its armour a tank was a safe thing to be in. I suppose we should have known that the army has a way of not always telling you things in the most tactful manner."

Eventually they were given passes to go home on a brief period of leave. "Although nothing was said I had a feeling that my family and friends had noticed a change in me, perhaps because I was constantly polishing my boots and kept calling my friends "orrible little men!" On completion of basic training, Richard was sent to Tidworth to join the 17/21 Lancers prior to going to Munster, in Germany, part of the British Army of the Rhine. This regiment was known as the "Death or Glory Boys" because of the famous Charge of the Light Brigade in the Crimean War. Formerly a cavalry regiment with a proud history, it had retained its high military standards and unique traditions. One that was rigorously upheld was striking silver skull and crossbones cap badge, which was never called a badge but a motto, and woe betide any man who called it a badge!

They travelled to Germany on the overnight ferry from Harwich to the Hook of Holland. "The SS Empire Wansbeck, a converted minesweeper, was a vessel that did not appear to specialise in super holiday cruises but more like bruise cruises! Having deposited our supper of bacon and fried bread kindly provided by the Catering Corps in bags 'for the use of' and thoughtfully supplied by the ship's crew, who obviously knew a thing or two about the North Sea, we were transferred to a waiting train and made our way through Holland to Munster. En route there were ample visible reminders of the battles fought in this area during World War II. In Munster they encountered a certain amount of hostility from some of the more elderly locals who had very recent memories of the bitter conflict they had lived through and, in some cases, taken part in.

This was the era of the 'Cold War', when the nations of the west stood face-to-face with the countries of the Communist Bloc, and a good deal of sabre-rattling went on. Richard's regiment were equipped with the Centurion, the latest British tank, armed with 20 pounder guns that were kept fully loaded with live rounds and maintained to a high state of battle readiness, just in case the enemy decided to attack. They never did so, deterred by the threat of all-out nuclear war, but our forces had to be ready at all times nevertheless. They received visits from government ministers such as Anthony Eden, and an American general who had been in the Korean War.

Being near Belsen at times, they were taken to the site of the notorious Nazi concentration camp, which Richard describes as "something I will never forget."

Once a year they went on home leave in England. This entailed a long journey by boat and train, which did not leave much time at home, but it was good to catch up on friends and family, if only briefly.

Reflecting on his experience of National Service, Richard said "It did us no harm. We went in as boys and came out as men, and, I'm sure, better and possibly wiser citizens."

John Cuttriss' National Service

Born in 1938 in Chesterfield, John Cuttriss almost managed to avoid National Service. After leaving school at 15, he became an apprentice painter and decorator. He was able to defer his call-up until he had gained his City and Guilds Certificate, and delayed his final exam by a year while the ending of National Service was being debated, but by September 1959 he could put it off no longer and received notification to attend Mansfield Medical Centre. He was passed as A1. Just a few months later National Service was abolished!

John's brother had done his service in the RAF, and strongly advised John to do the same. He was successful, and was sent for basic training to RAF Cardington, in Bedfordshire, where once the airship R101 had been housed in one of its two gigantic hangars. Here he was introduced to his new 'home', a long wooden hut containing 20 beds, 10 down each side with a room at the end for the corporal. He was initiated in the bizarre rituals of a recruit's life, such as folding one's bedclothes into a 'bed box'. This involved arranging three blankets and two sheets alternately and wrapping them into a fourth blanket so that it resembled a liquorice allsort. This had to be done meticulously every morning. He was issued with a uniform, a kitbag, a groundsheet for wearing in wet weather and various items for personal smartness including an item intriguingly referred to as a 'housewife.' This was a canvas bag containing a cotton reel, darning wool, needles, a bathplug (!) and a mushroom for darning socks. This last item was a salutary reminder to these young men that they would no longer be able to delegate such chores as sewing and darning to their mothers!

John now had to make a decision. He could serve the compulsory two years, but with his qualifications he could alternatively sign on for nine years as a painter and doper (an archaic term from the First World War, when biplanes were coated with dope to strengthen their fabric skins. By John's time a 'doper' sprayed aircraft and applied the markings and numbers). This would mean immediate promotion to corporal, with all the privileges that that entailed. Alternatively, he could serve for three years, followed by two further years in the reserves. This would considerably boost his weekly wage, to £3.10s (£3.50) a week instead of £1.8s (£1.40). Other benefits included a better quality uniform, extra leave and free travel warrants. He would also enjoy a higher status as a regular rather than a National Serviceman, who tended to be regarded as the lowest form of life. Although John was attracted to the nine-year option, his fiancée was not, and so he chose to sign on for three years as a teleprinter operator.

However, it would be some time before he got near a teleprinter. First there was ten weeks "square bashing" at RAF Bridgnorth, in Shropshire. As at Cardington, the airmen lived in wooden barrack huts which had to be kept scrupulously clean. Once a week there was "bull night" when every square inch of the hut had to be cleaned and polished ready for inspection. The incentive was the radio. There was only one between four huts, and the smartest one had the radio for a week. Interspersed with the drill were lectures on various topics, including sexual health. Unlike at Cardington, they were allowed out into the town, and were told to be careful to avoid the "Wolverhampton Wanderers". This was not a reference to local football supporters, but to predatory females who might leave the unwary airman with a medical condition he was not expecting!

John's hut were the best of the four drill units and received an unexpected reward by being chosen to line the route along Horseguards Parade for the visit in 1960 of General de Gaulle, the President of France. Unfortunately, this meant the cancellation of their passing-out parade, but they felt it was worth the disappointment for the honour of being involved in such an important state occasion.

Basic Training over, John was then posted to No3 Radio School, RAF Compton Bassett, in Wiltshire. Here the regime was more relaxed. Their days were no longer spent square bashing, but learning to touch type and getting acquainted with the teleprinter. Twelve weeks later he was on the move again, this time to RAF Scampton, in Lincolnshire, wartime home of the famous 617 'Dam Busters' Squadron. Here they practised Quick Readiness Alert (QRA), where the Vulcan bombers had to be ready to take off in four minutes in response to the threat of a Soviet nuclear attack. John's role in this was to receive, process and deliver signal instructions to pilots waiting in readiness.

Soon afterwards John was on the move again, this time to Pitreavie Castle in Scotland. This Victorian pile had been acquired by the RAF in the 1930s and was a joint Navy and RAF station. It was from here that the Battle of the Atlantic and the hunt for the Tirpitz had been planned during the war, and was now playing an important role in the Cold War as a communications centre. Here John became acquainted with the curious Naval practice of treating every shore station as though it was a ship. Leaving the camp was "going ashore", and catching a bus was "catching a liberty boat." Once John was reprimanded by a Naval officer for not "saluting the quarter deck", which was a flag atop a pile of whitewashed stones!

John discovered that you could exchange postings with another person so as to be nearer home, and he found a lad called Jock MacKenzie from Perth who had been posted to the North Regional Air Traffic Control Centre at Barton Hall, near Preston. A swap was arranged, and a few weeks later John was heading south to Preston while Jock took his place at Pitreavie Castle. He was now much nearer home, although the journey normally involved hitch hiking, as he could not afford the train fare. In those days anyone in uniform could easily get a lift (whereas today hitchhikers are hardly ever seen.) In fact, John got a regular lift with a sugar lorry that did deliveries between Preston and Chesterfield.

The billets were at nearby RAF Wheeton, Blackpool. Again they lived in wooden huts but there were no parades or guard duties, and they could come and go as they pleased. The work involved plotting the military and civilian aircraft along the various corridors, and although the regime was relaxed, the attitude was totally professional. He was there from September 1960 to April 1961, when he received notification of his next posting, this time overseas. He was to go to Rheindahlen, in Germany.

Rheindahlen was the communications centre for all NATO forces. It was the size of a small town and had shops, cafes, bars, a swimming pool and a cinema. The accommodation was quite luxurious compared to the Spartan huts that John had lived in before. The men lived five to a room, with showers and laundry facilities. The work involved sending and receiving teleprinter messages, most of which were of mundane, routine matters, though things hotted up considerably when the Berlin Wall went up in August 1961, and suddenly the prospect of the Third World War briefly loomed up. Sometimes the communications centre was dispersed and set up in an undisclosed destination, so as to be prepared for a possible war situation. During this time they lived under canvas.

John and his mates took advantage of free time to travel. They visited Dusseldorf, Amsterdam and Konigswinter, where they visited the famous 'Drachenfels', the ruined castle which overlooks the Rhine. Life was pleasant enough, but home and family still seemed a long way away, and letters from home were always eagerly received. John crossed off the days until demob, but even when he was finally discharged he still remained on the reserve. For the next two years he received one shilling and sixpence a day and for the final six months a shilling a day. In 1964 he had to attend a refresher course for two weeks at Plymouth. After that his National Service was finally over.

Although John had tried his best to avoid doing National Service, he found the experience enjoyable and beneficial. He did not regret his decision to sign up for three years rather than two; he may have lost out on civilian earnings but the extra year made his service easier to live through.

John has written a book, 'Destination Dusseldorf' about his three years in the RAF, from which I have drawn most of the information in this account. The book is available from the author, John Cuttress, telephone 01246-275110.

Epilogue

Needless to say, the people I interviewed for this project were all coming to the end of their lives. The youngest was 73, the oldest was 99. Some were in poor health and one passed away before this book was published. Yet what they all showed was a tremendous enthusiasm for what I was doing. They really wanted their stories told before it was too late, because they knew they had lived through a unique time in our history. Never before had there been such a sense of unity in the nation. Never before had the entire population – men, women and children – been so totally mobilised in the nation's cause.

Of course, it would be wrong to be over-sentimental. Whilst the vast majority of the population pulled together, there was that inevitable sub-strata of society who cared nothing for the common good and took advantage of the disruption of normal life to further their own ends. A thriving black market, organised by men known as 'spivs', surreptitiously provided goods (usually stolen) that were hard to come by, and looting of bombed property, very easy in the blackout, was a regular occurrence. Not all men could accept military discipline and went AWOL (absent without leave), preferring to spend the war years in hiding, at least until the police caught up with them. Others found ways of dodging conscription with spurious claims of medical incapacity.

With the exception of this minority, everybody willingly and uncomplainingly 'did their bit' for the country, and can now justifiably look back with pride on those extraordinary years. Had we not won the war, it does not bear thinking about what our lives today would be like under the most brutal, merciless and evil regime in history. As it was, those of us who came along afterwards were not only spared this ghastly fate but were able to live our lives in peace and ever-growing prosperity. We owe them an incalculable debt. Not for nothing have they been called 'The Greatest Generation'.

I hope that in writing this book I have gone some way to repaying them.

About the Author

Malcolm Cowper grew up in South Wales but spent most of his adult lfe teaching English in Derbyshire. Now retired, he divides his time between walking in the beautiful Peak District and being a volunteer with the Samaritans.